CONFLICT
IN THE
BEAUTIFUL CITY
THE SERPENT EXPOSED

Phillip S. Smith III

Copyright © 2016 by Phillip S. Smith III

CONFLICT IN THE BEAUTIFUL CITY
THE SERPENT EXPOSED
by Phillip S. Smith III

Printed in the United States of America.

ISBN 9781498469432

All rights reserved solely by the author. The author guarantees all contents are original and do not infringe upon the legal rights of any other person or work. No part of this book may be reproduced in any form without the permission of the author. The views expressed in this book are not necessarily those of the publisher.

www.xulonpress.com

Cedar Falls, USA was a small Midwestern town which was originally populated with a lot of Indians. In fact, this was their land a long time ago. One could go out to the Indian mounds and still find shards, pottery, arrowheads, spear heads, and many other artifacts. One area had a lot of well preserved bones that had been there for centuries. Many of the Indian relics were on display in the local museum including a very well preserved totem pole of which no one knew of its origin. The so called myths behind the totem pole was that the Indians would dance around it, pray to it, and receive instructions for war, sex, marriage, rain, and the future. When instructions would come, there would be a pall in the air, and a darkness would settle over the whole tribe while they awaited the witch doctor's instructions he got from the dark cloud. Myths had it that the witch doctor controlled everybody's life from the day they were born till the day they died. It was believed by the old timers in town that there was a secret burial site, and that the totem still existed. The truth was that most totem poles were located in Alaska and in British Columbia, and were never really worshipped by the Indians. Early missionaries traveling west attached shamanism to the totems and it stuck.

1
FAMILY

Cedar Falls was typical of a lot of small towns in the USA. It had a main street with many vibrant stores, a mayor/council type government, a local stock broker, a good community bank with plenty of reserves, a cinema that would hold up to 100 people at a time, a small town news paper, and the typical Methodist, Baptist, Catholic, and Pentecostal churches on major corners. New housing starts were flourishing as oil and gas was been fracted from under ground, and oil companies were paying big bucks to drill. As a result, families were moving in to take advantage of the booming economy. Many skilled oil field laborers were infiltrating the area which was once a bountiful agricultural area. Wheat and corn fields which once dominated the landscape were now being replaced with oil derricks and pumps.

It rained that night and high winds ripped some of the shingles off the roofs. Buck got up and put buckets under the drips and then went back to bed. He arose about 6:30 and surveyed the damage. "Looks like we not only have shingles missing and a serious leak, but we also have some electrical damage where water got in some of the electrical lines", he told Susie. "We need somebody that knows what they are doing. I'm going down to the lumber company to get some shingles, and stop by Bennie's and get a haircut. In the meantime, see if you can find someone, preferably a good handyman to come out and make repairs."

On a given day, people were seen driving into town in their trucks, buses, and RV's or even just walking to get there. On one such day, a man showed up strolling through downtown with his overalls, brogans, T-Shirt, a pull-on light blue cover up shirt, and a ball cap which said Florida State on the crest. His hair was hanging out of his ball cap as he passed Bennie White's barber shop. He had a weathered face and well tanned arms. Bennie was standing outside smoking a cigarette when Joe walked by.
"Looks like you need a haircut, stranger," Bennie said nonchalantly.
"Yup," replied the stranger. "But, I don't have any money right now. I need to get some carpentry work. Reckon where I might look if you don't mind me asking?"
Bennie said, "It just happens to be we just had a major storm blow through here, and a lot of folks got wind and hail, and tree damage to their homes. I just talked to Buck Merriman this morning and he was looking for someone who was a handyman."
"Where might I find him?" Joe asked.
"Go down about 3 blocks, take a right and go one mile and he's on the right. He lives in a really nice home with red brick and huge white pillars in front. By the way, what is your name, stranger?"
"Joe!"
"Joe, huh? What is your last name?"
"It's just Joe."
"I guess you're from Florida?" Queried Bennie.
"I am, but how did you know?"
"It's your cap. It says Florida State on it."
"Ha Ha Ha!" laughed Joe. "It gave me away didn't it? Ok, got to go see if I can make a couple a' bucks. I got just enough to get me a motel room for about 3 days. Gonna' go get a room and head out. See you later, Bennie."
"Yeah, see you Joe."

Buck called Susie and told her that Bennie had met a new man who was a carpenter named Joe, but he wasn't sure where he was. Susie got on the phone then and called around to some of her friends in the country club. She heard there was a new man in town named Joe who did all kinds of repairs. It must be the same man. And he was staying at the only motel in Cedar Falls. He was, and according to reports not expensive. Not that it made any difference to Susie and Buck as they were very well to do. Buck made an extremely good living in sales working for an international sales company. Buck knew three languages and was very valuable.

News really traveled fast in Cedar Falls. You could not spit on the sidewalk without somebody noticing. And so it was with this stranger walking through town. Everybody knew he was there.

Susie had a frugal spirit and liked to make good deals just like her mother. She looked up the number of the motel to see if the stranger was in. The phone rang five times. Finally a voice at the other end answered, "Hello".

Brad was a good boy, but he had a stubborn streak. That was the hard part for his parents, Buck and Susie. They just simply did not know how to break Brad of his insubordination. He made good grades, he was popular in school, and he was very athletic being the star quarterback of Cedar Falls' Panthers and the star pitcher of the Cedar Falls' Panther's baseball team. Every body liked him, but when it came to obeying his parents, he fell short. They tried to reason in their minds that he had a lot of other good attributes, and that he was well liked by all. Why, he was not all bad. In fact, he had more good in him. After all, Buck and Susie were very well off and gave Brad everything. His graduation gift was a brand new red, Ford Mustang, and he had a lifetime membership at the Cedar Falls Country Club. This was his last year in high school and he was graduating valedictorian of his class. Everything seemed to be going well, but there was that nagging in their spirit that said Brad needed to get his stubbornness under control.

Rev. John from the Methodist Church called and asked Brad if he wanted to go on a mission trip to the Navajo Indians in Arizona the summer after he graduated, which Brad gladly accepted. Maybe, just maybe this was the event that was to bring about a life change in Brad.

Buck and Susie were elated. And Brad seemed to be excited about the trip. The "why" nobody knew, but they were glad.

Brad and Amy had been constant companions since the 10th grade. Lately, they had been discussing marriage. It was a match made in heaven. When Amy found out Brad was going to minister to the Navajo Indians, she wanted to go. Her parents tried to talk her out of it, but she was insistent. After all, it was a spiritual event, and it would be good for all. Her parents could not refuse.

Brad slid behind the wheel of his new red Mustang. He liked the feel of the gold leather seats, the look of the wood grain dash, and floor mounted automatic transmission. He got this devilish grin on his face when he rubbed his hands across the steering wheel and on the dash. He cranked the engine for the first time. The mufflers had a loud sound, one of those "varooom" when he pressed on the accelerator. "Ahhh", he said, "this is sweet." Suddenly, he heard a flutter, then he saw a dark figure pass by his vision. After he blinked his eyes and looked, there was nothing there, or so he thought. Now, for a test drive. Brad eased his new mean machine out into the lazy street in front of his parent's house. He rolled down to the intersection at the stop sign. Going right and left was a four lane thoroughfare where he could really give that baby a good test drive. Suddenly, he removed his foot from the brake and engaged the accelerator spinning and sliding onto the thoroughfare. Faster and faster he went. It was exhilarating. He was doing 60 before he knew it, then 70. He was passing cars like they were standing still. He still had pedal, and pressed down. The speedometer showed 90 then 100. He came to a group of cars that had slowed to a crawl because of a wreck ahead. He pulled off the thoroughfare onto a side road, and casually rode back home with one hand on the steering wheel and his other arm hanging out the window feeling like a king. He was on top of the world.

The trip to Arizona was only a week away, and Brad and Amy both needed to pack, make airline reservations, and coordinate their week with the pastor's schedule. They were busy getting arrangements made when Brad felt the icy presence of a hand around his neck and strong sensation around his chest like he was being crushed by a boa constrictor. Suddenly, Amy bounced into the room, giggling and shouting because of the trip they were going on together. The icy hand and the crushing sensation left as quickly as it came. Amy quickly glanced at Brad, and saw that his face was ashen white.

"What is wrong?" she asked.

Brad, not wanting to seem like a "sissy" in front of his girl friend, said, he had just eaten some pizza and it must be indigestion. Although Brad blew it off, he knew it was more than that.

It was six days before departure. Everyone was in a celebratory mood, especially Brad and Amy. They couldn't wait for marriage. They had been having regular sex since the 10th grade. She was smart enough to get birth control pills early in her sophomore year so they wouldn't have to worry about an unwanted pregnancy. Today was really special. Making love to Brad was really special, and she could not wait to get married to make all this romanticism legal.

Buck and Susie were so happy. Brad and Amy had both graduated with great honors, scholarships to major colleges were on their desk, and Brad was about to get married to his childhood sweetheart. Life could not be better. They reveled that their son had done so well in high school both in the class room and on the field. Because of their wealth and prestige, they felt like that they had been able to afford the best for Brad and make a champion out of him. But, still there was that nagging, persistent pressure saying something was wrong. They again reasoned, "how could one bad attribute spoil all the other good attributes?"

Brad and Amy, in the meantime were still in a jubilant mood. In just a few days, they were to go on the trip of a lifetime, at least to them, and they had talked about their future marriage, having kids, and making a good life together. There was truly joy in the camp everywhere. The future held exceedingly great promises for them both. They went outside to enjoy the sunshine and talk about what they would name their kids, where they would live, and what they would do for the rest of their life. The future looked bright.

Suddenly, a wind began to kick up. Sand began to twist in a small funnel and come toward them. A dark cloud immediately appeared, and a sense of evil pervaded over them. Twisting debris came at them slowly turning, ever advancing, menacingly darting at them.

Amy shouted, "Jesus!", and immediately all was quite. No more twisting wind, no more clouds, no more presence of danger.
"What was that?" Brad asked.
Amy said, "It had to be an evil spirit trying to dissuade us from going on this trip."
"Bah!" exclaimed Brad. I don't believe in all that silly stuff. Though Brad knew the rites and ceremonies of the Methodist Church and plenty of religion tossed in, he had never really noticed a spirit world like Amy was talking about. Amy went out of preference to a local "Charismatic" home meeting where she learned about warfare in the spirit, and about spiritual wickedness. It was not a coincidence to her. She had personally witnessed people being delivered from demonic spirits, and closely observed as their lives went from dark to light.

The day of departure was getting near. Rev. Goodman had called Brad. Amy, in the meantime was going to meet them at the airport. Buck and Susie had packed some treats for Brad to take on the trip thinking they may not be able to get any in the desert.

Brad was insistent on going to pick up Amy at her home in his new Mustang to show her how it drove.
Susie said, "Now Brad, drive under the speed limit and stop at all the stop signs. Be careful and watch what you are doing. That is a new car and it is really fast, so your father and I want you to be careful."
"Screw you," Brad thought, "this thing is not designed to go slow."

When Brad got to Amy's house, he was so excited as well as was Amy. Quickly, he loaded her in his chariot. Like a gentleman, he opened the door for her to get in the passenger side, and helped her fasten her seat belt. He ran around the front of the car, and jumped behind the wheel. Varoom, went the engine when he started it up. "Hot dog, how do you like that sound?" he shouted. "Is that awesome or what?" Before he could engage the transmission, he felt an ominous presence on his shoulder.
"Faster!" it whispered.

Brad engaged the transmission and put his foot on the accelerator. Fast was the order of the day. He spun out leaving rock and gravel and a shroud of dust 20' high. He hollered, "This is the beginning of the rest of my life." Faster and faster he drove.

Amy said, "Brad, slow down!" but he only went faster. "Please slow down!" she said.

But, Brad could not hear her. He had turned the music up loud, and he heard only the words "Faster, Faster!" in his ears. By now, the voice in his ear was louder than ever, the music was at a crescendo and the evil presence had taken over his mind and body. " F a s t e r ! " it said, "Faster!"

He was going 60, then 70, then 80.

All the time Amy was saying, "Brad, please slow down!"
But, her words were drowned out by the other voices taking precedence in Brad's ear. His adrenaline had kicked in and that stubborn streak had taken control of his faculties. In a flash, Brad saw something out of the corner of his eye. It was a car that had tried to go through a stop sign. But Brad was going too fast to slow down or brake... there was no time to react. BAM-M-M-M! It was a head on collision for Brad. His car went hurtling through the air and rolled several times before it came to a stop on its side.

Ambulances, fire trucks, and police cars were on the scene in less than 10 minutes. The car that came out of the side road was damaged, but the four teenagers inside were only slightly injured. The ambulance picked them up and took them to the hospital for treatment.

"There are two of them in that little red mustang." said Kelly Vargas, the town Sheriff. "I think the girl is alive, but it looks like the driver is dead."

As the EMT's were pulling Amy out of the car, Joe happened to be walking by the wreck on the way to Buck's house. They put Amy in a neck brace then on a stretcher to take her to the hospital. They had to cut Brad out of the vehicle. It was crushed from front to back. Joe, in the meantime walked over to the stretcher before it was put in the ambulance, looked down at Amy, and touched her arm.

"Hey", shouted the EMT's, "get away from there".

Joe then walked over to the once beautiful mustang. It was now a pile of junk metal, twisted and gnarled from the wreck. They had just cut Brad's lifeless body out of the car. For a moment, time stopped. Brad's body was placed on the gurney, and they pulled a sheet over his head. The EMT's walked away briefly to talk with the Sheriff. Joe walked quickly up and touched the gurney with his left hand and put his right hand on the sheet where Brad's head was.

Again, the EMT's hollered, "Get away from there". Joe shook his head, then turned and walked slowly away. He had to go get some carpentry work.

The EMT's took Amy to the hospital to be treated and examined for other injuries she might have sustained from the wreck. Best guess was she broke her neck and would be forever paralyzed. The other EMT's loaded Brad in their ambulance to take him to the morgue. "Poor guy!" said one of the EMT's to the other. "Did you know he not only was the team quarterback for the Panthers, but he was the star pitcher for their baseball team and he was valedictorian of his graduating class. What a way to end your life!"

The "Morgue" was a 2-story, dark red, brick building with a basement. It had vines growing up each side and along the windows. It had not had any maintenance in over 30 years, and it was really looking weathered and eerie. Some of the window panes were broken and had duct tape over the cracks. Kids obviously had taken target practice at the windows with their BB-guns, and managed to crack many of them.

The ambulance backed up to the entrance door. The EMT's got out, opened the double doors, pulled the gurney down, locked the rollers in place, loaded Brad's lifeless body, unlocked the rollers, and began to enter the "Morgue". It was musty smelling in the hall, and it began to smell of chemicals and formaldehyde as they went toward the main holding room. The chief coroner, Dr. Everett Ellis met them at the doors and held them open to let them in.

"Take the body over by the examination station," he said. Dr. Ellis always did an external exam by feeling of the feet and the legs and the hands and arms. The body was cold as ice. Dr. Ellis took the sheet and slowly but methodically folded it down off Brad's face onto his stomach. He reached for his saw to split the chest to begin the autopsy. The saw would not come on. When he realized the saw wouldn't work, he bent down and saw it was unplugged from the wall. Reaching out to plug it in, he sensed movement from the operating table. Looking up, he saw Brad's eyes fly open like an owl's when he was going to hoot. Suddenly, Brad raised up on the table from the waist.

He looked at Dr. Ellis and said, "I sure am hungry, where am I?" Brad uncovered himself from the sheet, and slid off the table. He realized he was naked, and said, "What's going on here?" Dr. Ellis had never seen anything like this in all his 30 years of being the county coroner.

He stammered, "How did-d-d-d-d you do that?"

"Do what?" Brad exclaimed.

"How did you come back to life. Just a few moments ago, you were dead as a hammer and ice cold. And you've been dead for over 2 hours now. Do you remember anything that happened to you?"

Brad said, "Yes, I remember flying down the highway and having a head on collision. I remember looking at Amy, and saying "God, don't let anything happen to Amy! And then nothing. Then, what seemed like an eternity, I watched as my whole life passed before me in an instant. I felt this great comforting hand on my forehead, and then a great white light so brilliant that I could not look upon it. Then a voice came," "Peace, and rest a moment for everything is going to be all right. Your life is in my hands." As quickly as it came, it went, and everything was cold and dark until just now. Again, another voice said, "Rise and walk, Brad!" "So here I am. Can you explain all that Dr. Ellis? And where are my clothes? It is cold in here."

Dr. Ellis ran over to the stock room and got Brad some hospital togs. "Here, put these on." he said. Brad quickly dressed and prepared to leave.

Then he turned to Dr. Ellis, "I don't suppose my new car is driveable, is it, Dr. Ellis?"

"No, Brad, I'm afraid it is all a pile of twisted metal. It's not coming back to life like you."

Amy was weeping and preparing to go to the funeral home as she sat in a wheel chair when she got the call from the coroner's office. She had been preparing to see her future husband laid out in a casket with his Sunday best.

"Amy!" the voice said on the other end of the line, "This is Dr. Ellis. I have some good news and some bad news for you. The good news is that Brad is not dead, but fully alive and trying to leave the morgue. The bad news is his mustang is totaled and he doesn't have a ride."

The news hit Amy right in the pit of her stomach and raced through her body like lightning. She jumped up from the wheel chair, then fell down on her knees, doubled her fist in a ball, pumped her arm and screamed to the top of her lungs, "YES-S-S-!"

All of their plans for the future previously had been dashed. They would not get married, would not have any children, and would not live the good life. And, Amy would require rehabilitation for the next six months before she could function again. But, all that changed in an instant. "How," she thought, "could Brad be alive?" The last time she saw him, he was not breathing and she had heard the EMT's pronounce the death sentence on him. "Dr. Ellis," she said after gaining her composure, "What do you attribute to Brad coming back from the dead? I saw him myself. There was no life in him."

Dr. Ellis just shrugged his shoulders though she could not see, and said, "All I can tell you is that we have witnessed a notable miracle here today, Amy." But, Amy's miracle was no less notable. It was thought she would be paralyzed for life, but there she was arising from her wheel chair, standing and walking and moving as if nothing had ever happened.

Buck and Susie were devastated and sobbed profusely over their son after hearing the news. Their hope and aspirations for the almost perfect son was obliterated, the longing for grandchildren to carry on the family name was no more, and the picture perfect couple would never have a life together.

Then Dr. Ellis called. Susie answered. "Susie, this is Dr. Ellis. I have some good news," he said. "HE'S ALIVE!" Dr. Ellis proclaimed. "HE'S ALIVE!" BRAD IS ALIVE! He said again thinking she may not have understood him. Over the phone, he could hear them shouting. Susie grabbed Buck and began to dance and fling him all over the room. It was a joyous moment!

Amy had gone down to the morgue to pick Brad up and met Buck and Susie going in before her. They hugged and spun around as "one" in the hall all the way to the main autopsy room. As they entered the room, there was Brad grinning sheepishly as if nothing had ever gone wrong. They all went over and gave him a group hug. Amy heard a sound and looked up. Above the operating table arose a dark object as if sneering at her, and like a whirlwind, it was gone.

Buck and Susie needed answers, so after a much long and heated discussion, they decided to go see their pastor. Two days later, their appointment brought them to the door of the pastor's office. Lightly they knocked.

"Come in", declared the cool voice within. Slowly, they entered the pastor's chamber. The walls were stained cherry and the floors were a brown granite tile 18" square. It had a huge library on one side full of inspirational books, maps, charts and bibles of all kinds. On the other side was a 10' mirror decorated on the sides, top and bottom with figures of golden angels playing on streets of gold. Behind the pastors desk was a huge credenza and shelving rising to the ceiling with all manner of artifacts from all over the world. His desk was a splendid work made of the finest ash, and stained a dark cherry. It was adorned with a special pen with ornate holder all bought in the holy land on his last trip. Next to it, he also had a curved bladed knife with a partially red stained bone handle and a skull on the end he had gotten from Haiti on a mission trip 15 years ago. His chair was of a dark brown leather which swiveled and was well padded on the back, as well as were the seat and the arms. In one corner was a plain closet with an external lock on the door. Buck and Susie felt that they had entered the room of a great corporate CEO or even the president himself. They were so in awe, they could not speak.

"Well, what is the nature of your visit"?, the pastor asked. "We have come to talk to you about the accident that Brad had," Susie blurted.

"I see, and what is your question?"

Susie continued, "Brad was at the top of his class, a great athlete, loved by all, and had a great future. This wreck could have been fatal. He was going on this mission trip for God, so why did he have the accident, and how do you explain that he was dead and is now alive? And Amy could have been paralyzed for life, but she looks and walks and talks as if nothing at all has happened."

"Well, there is a lot of things you don't understand," the pastor said.

"We know and that is why we are here, to get answers."

The pastor went on, "the bible says it is appointed unto men once to die and then the judgment. He escaped death. It just was not his time. That's it."

"That's it?" Susie questioned.

"Yep, that's it. Any other questions?"

"No," Buck and Susie said in unison, "that will be all." When they got up to leave, a specter appeared behind the pastor's chair and slowly began to disappear into the cabinets behind his chair. With a last flit, it was gone.

"Did you see that?" Susie whispered to Buck as they left the pastor's office.

"I saw it." said Buck, "but I'm not going back to ask the pastor." I'm not interested in any more short answers that don't solve the problem or answer my questions. And, I'm sure not going to ask about that thingggg that we just saw. I probably don't want to know."

"Where do you think we ought to go?" Susie questioned.

"I think we need to go see Amy."

Buck and Susie had not been intimate in several days. Perhaps it was because of Brad's wreck or maybe she was just on her period, but Buck was feeling really frustrated. He knew just the remedy. In fact, it was his remedy for everything, SEX! Buck loved sex, and had ever since he lost his virginity at 14. All his girl friends loved him because of his prowess. Buck didn't have many days go by without a sample, that is until he got married.

Buck knew just what he needed, and that was to go see Ruby Dixon, the town tramp. Ruby was a good looking woman, had a great body, and she really knew how to ply her trade. They had several encounters, and today would be a great stress reliever with Ruby. On entering her condo, Buck knew he was at the right place at the right time. Ruby was dressed in a flimsy negligee, had some Estee Lauder's "Pleasures" and smelled awesome. Elvis Presley was singing on her Ipod in the background, "It's now or never," and the mood was set. It was alright with the world.

The next day, Susie called Amy to get some answers to all the mysterious things that had been happening. Amy immediately called her pastor and arranged a meeting. Jimmy Hawkins didn't look like a minister. He didn't dress the part, he didn't have a big office like Pastor John Goodman, and he didn't have a religious gasp. In fact, he just looked and talked normal, and his office was his living room in his house. As Buck and Susie walked in, they were met with a very warm welcome, and invited to sit. Ashley, Jimmy's wife, came in and brought iced tea for everyone. They seemed so warm and... well.... friendly. It was strange talking to someone who was in ministry who didn't have a religious air about them.

After everyone got settled and got their drinks, Jimmy said, "Amy told me a little about what has been going on in the last few days, but I'm not sure what you need. What questions can I answer for you.... if I can?"

Buck was totally amazed at Jimmy's humility. He didn't even profess to know everything like other ministers in the community. "I'm puzzled!" said Buck. "Number one, why did Brad have this wreck, number two, both Brad and Amy appeared to be almost destroyed, Amy seemed apparently paralyzed, and Brad was pronounced dead and taken to the morgue. As you can see, they are both perfect. It doesn't even make sense. My wife and I have never seen anything like this before, nor have any of our friends, and the doctors and coroner are totally amazed. How can this my son be dead, but then suddenly be alive?"

Jimmy was slow to answer, "Mr. Merriman,"

"Please call me Buck."

"Buck, do you believe in miracles?"

"Actually, we don't.' said Buck. "My pastor told me miracles passed away with the apostles. And besides that, as far as I know, I have never witnessed one."

Jimmy drawled, "Well-l-l-l, I guess we can safely say that you have now. Buck, you must know that Brad has a destiny ahead of him and it was not his time to go. The same goes for Amy. Her destiny is wrapped up in Brad, and the two of them have great potential in the Kingdom of God."

"Excuse me,' Buck said, "but what has the Kingdom of God got to do with these so called miracles?"

"Everything!" replied Jimmy. "Everything!" God has chosen them from their mother's womb, even from the foundation of the world. He has set a seal on them that they should not perish from this earth until their assignment is done."

"Man, I have never heard anyone talk like this," said Buck, "In fact, I didn't even have the foggiest notion anything like you said even existed except in bible stories." Susie was steadily shaking her head in agreement in one moment then shaking her head in disbelief the next.

"How can these things be?" Susie shot back. "He is just my baby boy."

"That is exactly what Mary thought after her baby was grown and starting doing miracles. It was just as incredulous to her as this is to y'all. Brad has a calling on his life, and God is going to bring it to fruition. I've talked to Amy many times about him, and I believe I have a good picture of his calling. He only has one problem."

"What is that?" Susie wanted to know.

"It appears he is stubborn and has a spirit of rebellion," Jimmy said. "It was likely the reason he had the wreck in the first place. If I were a betting man, I would bet y'all told him to drive that new car carefully."

"Yes, but how did you know?" Susie asked.

"Amy has told me all about Brad's good points as well as his downsides. The main one being that he doesn't listen or obey anything you say. You've given him everything he has ever wanted, and he has never been disciplined or restrained for any reason. You are fortunate that he has so much drive and the desire to excel. Otherwise, he might wind up a skid row bum. It might be a little late to start the discipline process, but God has plans for him, and this wreck may create a little humility and more "yes, sirs" and "yes, ma'ams in his life."

"I don't believe I have ever had anybody talk to me the way you have, Pastor, but I can't say me and my wife don't deserve it. For sure, from this day and forward, we can and will be a little more circumspect toward our son. Though I don't know what it is, I must say we want him to fulfill his calling."

"Is there anything else I can help you with?" Jimmy asked.

"No, I think we have our questions answered for now, and maybe just maybe we got a more than we bargained for. Thank you, Pastor!"

"Look, I have some errands to run," said Susie.

"Buck, could you stay a little longer? I have something I want to run by you." "Sure!" said Buck.

Susie left, Ashley had to go to town, and Buck and Jimmy were left alone in the living room.

"What's up, Pastor? Buck questioned.

"Buck, I'm no prophet, but God has shown me that you have some serious lust issues if you don't mind me speaking frankly. He also showed me you could lose your wife and family if you don't get it in control. I know you don't want to lose your beautiful wife and the respect of your son, so I'm just putting this out there for you to perk on. I don't have mastery over your soul, and I'm not trying to tell you what to do, and I haven't heard anything on the street. This is just between me, you, and God." Buck couldn't speak. How, he thought could anyone know about his deep dark secrets and his uncontrollable lust?

He cleared his throat, "Thanks, Pastor!" and quickly left his home.

Brad and Susie met up that evening to talk about the recent almost tragedies they had gone through. The day to go on the mission trip had come and gone. Pastor Goodman never said a word to them, but just left very mysteriously. It appeared to Brad that he could have at least inquired as to his well being. After all, Brad was a member of his church, and his parents were faithful church goers and good tithers.

"Amy, do you remember anything about that wreck? Asked Brad.

"The only thing I can remember was that I could open my eyes, but none of my body would move. And, I remember the EMT's putting a brace around my neck, lifting me onto the stretcher, and just laying there for a minute. Someone came up to me in overalls and touched my hand. As soon as he did, I could wiggle my toes and fingers. Then I was carried away by the ambulance. What did you remember?"

"Nothing, absolutely nothing," said Brad. "But, when I got to the morgue, a bright light shone in my eyes, and I shot up like a rocket. It was really weird. I noticed I was cold like ice for a moment, then I began to warm up quickly. You got any clues as to what happened?

"Brad, I think God has something special for your life. You are alive for that reason. How do you feel overall?"

"I feel different, like something has changed me inside. My car is shot to hell and back, and I think I need to go apologize to my parents. And you know me, I never apologize.... to no one. I mean it, Amy, I'm feeling really remorseful. I've never felt like this before."

"Brad, we've had this conversation before, but I want to ask you again, do you think you are saved, or have you ever asked Christ in your heart? I mean really!

I don't think so, Amy, but if I had died, I would be in Hell today, wouldn't I?

"You know, Brad, you are an awesome guy with great qualities, but none of those qualities will get you in heaven. I am so thankful you got one more chance. And, yes, you would be in Hell if Jesus was not your Lord. This might be a real good time to take care of that little problem. What do you think?"

"What do I do? Brad asked.

"Just invite him into your heart. It's that simple. Just close your eyes...

"WOW! Exclaimed Brad. I felt him. I just got saved. I know I did. Man, this is awesome. I feel fresh, clean, like a new born babe. It seems like I am floating. I didn't know the chains of sin could be so heavy."
"GLORY!" Where did that come from? I've never said that before."

Brad and Amy got in Amy's car to go talk to Brad's parents. "You know, Amy, I am completely changed. I sense everything in me has been turned upside down, or right side up depending from which angle you see this. I'm thinking we might not ought to have any more sex until we get married."

"Brad, I'm a Christian, too, you know."

"I know," said Brad, "I'm not saying you are not but, I'm thinking we just need to wait. That's all I'm saying. It just seems right."

"I agree, but we might ought to move the wedding up on the calendar. I don't know if I can wait till the end of July."

Brad busted through the door, and hollered, "Dad, Dad, Mom, Mom, where are y'all?"

"In the kitchen, son. What's up?"

"Dad, Mom, y'all have been the best Mom and Dad anybody could ask for. I know I have not been easy to raise, in fact, I have been downright rebellious and stubborn. I see that now. The wreck made me realize how close we are to death on any given day. Please, forgive me for being such a pain all these 18 years! I promise, I will be different from now on. And, I am so sorry about the mustang."

Buck and Susie were in shock. Who was this standing in front of them? It was a different person for sure. In unison, they said, "We forgive you, Son. We've just always wanted the best for you."

"I know, Dad and Mom. There is something else I have to tell you. I just got saved. I'm not sure what all that means just yet, but I know I'm changed and changed for good. I'm all beside myself. Everything is giddy inside, and I have this great joy I can't even explain. Is that good or what?"

Susie said, "Brad, I am so happy for you." Buck just stood there with his eyes bugged out in total amazement. He didn't know what being saved was exactly, though he heard his Pastor talk about it. It seems like if you were a member of the Methodist Church you were saved, or so he said. Now, he was looking at his number one son and saw first hand what saved was. It was amazing.

Early the next day, Buck pulled his golf cart up on the driving range at the country club to bust a few balls. He felt really tense inside. He got out of the cart, teed up, and got ready to drive that ball as far as he could. But, before he could swing, he started to weep, then cry, then he began to sob out loud. He couldn't control it. What is going on with me? He pondered. He heard a hammer nailing. He turned and saw the new carpenter in town putting shingles on the club house. Suddenly, their eyes met, and Buck felt really ashamed. Joe's stare was like a hot welding rod piercing his eyes and going to the depths of his soul. His legs began to wobble, and he fell to his knees. Sobbing uncontrollably now, he sputtered, "Help me, Lord!" What seemed like a only a moment, then in a flash, someone had reached down and grabbed his hand to pull him up.

"Rise", he said. It was Joe the carpenter. How could he have gotten down off that roof and walked 50 yards that quick, he opined? But there he was. Buck stood, but felt a fire consume his being. Joe walked away out of his sight. Buck could only think, "Was this what Brad was talking about, being saved?" He knew at that moment he was a new man, that he would be a better husband and dad, and that he would clean his life up from that point on. No more dabbling in cistern that was not mine. The thought occurred to him…I'm not going to that Methodist Church anymore, but I am going to Amy's Charismatic home group.

The next day, Buck was walking down Main Street when he heard the bells ring at the Catholic Church. When he looked up at the bell tower, he saw something he had never seen before. It was a dark object sitting on top of the steeple. The sun was in his eyes, so he thought he was seeing things at first. But, as he squinted and shaded his eyes, it became apparent. The creature looked like one of those ancient Gargoyles with pointed ears, long fingers and nails, and his feet had talons. His eyes were blood red and he was staring right at him. He appeared to have wings, but on second glance they seemed to disappear. His tail was long and pointed at the end. The creature lifted himself off the tower and flew right over his head glaring the whole time, then it disappeared into the horizon. Buck had the eeriest feeling of darkness and impending doom. What was that thing? he thought. Inside the church, Father Bordelon was making plans for the next mass. He had a couple of new altar boys he wanted to break in, and he was planning on meeting with them and their parents the next day. His desk was cluttered with prayer beads, a statue of Mary holding the baby Jesus, several other Catholic objects of reverence. Behind his desk was a wooden cross about 3' tall with Jesus hanging on it. The walls had pictures of the Pope, some of the Saints of old, and some religious prints of oil paintings by High Renaissance artists, such as Leonardo da Vinci, Michelangelo, and Raphael that he obtained the last time he was in Milan. Michelangelo emanated creative power, conceiving vast projects that drew for inspiration on the human body as the ultimate vehicle for emotional expression; Raphael created works that perfectly expressed the classical spirit—harmonious, beautiful, and serene. Each one of the prints made him feel...well, sensual. In the bottom drawer of his desk was a 22 LR Rimfire–Smith & Wesson. He used it primarily to take target practice to relieve stress. It was never in his mind to use it for self defense.

That evening, Buck and Susie decided to go to a home meeting at Pastor Jimmy's house which Amy invited them to. Buck was beside himself. Brad and Amy were already there when they walked in. Brad looked at his Dad, and said, "Dad, what has happened to you? I have never seen you look so happy and shiny." Buck looked at Brad and said, "Well, Son, I guess you are not the only one that can get saved. I had an awesome experience at the golf course."

"At the golf course? Quizzed Brad.
"Yep!" I'll explain later.

In the meantime, about 15 more participants came in, some sat on the couch, some in chairs and some on the floor. Jimmy started playing the guitar, and Ashley begin to sing, What A Mighty God We Serve. After a lively song service which neither Buck nor Brad had ever experienced, Jimmy had everyone sit down for the word. "But, before we have the word," he said, "Does anyone here have a testimony they would like to share?"

Simultaneously, Brad and Buck both jumped up and said, "I do!" There was such an anointing in the room after they got through telling of their conversions. Everyone one was ecstatic and began to applaud. Brad and Buck had never seen or heard of anyone being applauded for having a spiritual experience. Jimmy gave an awesome lesson on powers and principalities to which when he was finished, everyone again applauded.

"Anyone have any questions? Asked Jimmy. "Yes!" Buck emphatically replied. "Today, I was walking by the Catholic Church and saw what looked like a Gargoyle which glared at me then seemed to fly away. Surely, I was hallucinating."

Jimmy then began to expound on the word saying there were positively powers, and principalities, and rulers of darkness and spiritual wickedness in high places.

"Most certainly they can't be here, can they?" Buck asked. "This is Cedar Falls! Some folks think it is like the sleepy little town on television called Mayberry."

"They are everywhere." Jimmy replied. "Wherever there are people, there are spirits." "They lie, they steal, they destroy, they make innuendos, they tempt the baser man, they deceive, and they appeal to every kind of lust, and they kill as you may well already know. Oh, yes, they are real," said Jimmy.

"Where are they located?" Buck asked.

"They are in every stream of society, churches, economics, education, government, families, arts and media." replied Jimmy.

"You mean churches?"

"I certainly do. Where did you find the Gargoyle?"

"On top of the Catholic Church. And, oh, yes, Susie and I saw something rise up over Pastor Goodman's desk."

Brad chimed in, "I saw some dark objects on a couple of occasions myself. You think that might have been evil spirits?

"I sure do," Jimmy said. "Like I said, they are everywhere. You do not have to fear them for Jesus has rendered the devil and all his hierarchy helpless at the cross."

"Well, that is good news," remarked Brad.

Susie jumped in, "How do we fight them and help other people fight them? There may be a few who do not know what is going on."

"A few?" Jimmy countered. "A few?" It's been my experience that there are many who are totally oblivious to the spiritual battles surrounding their lives."

When Buck and Susie got home, Buck was feeling repentant. "Susie, there are some things I need to confess to you."

Susie held her hand up, "I already know. You don't think I have lived these 19 years with you and not know everything about you, do you? I have never challenged you on anything, but I have prayed, and today, God has answered my prayers. If God can forgive you, who am I that can do less. No need to iterate every sin. I know most of them. And so you will know, after this day, I will never bring up your past to you at all.... Ever!"

Buck grabbed her hands and held them in his, then he began to weep profusely. Then he grabbed her shoulders and pulled her to his chest and hugged oh so deep. "Thank you, Thank you, honey!" He said. "You have no clue what you just have done for me."

Susie had been a nominal Christian since she was 12 years old. With all the miracles that had happened within the last few weeks, and the salvation of her husband and son, she went deeper. She had Jimmy and Ashley to pray for her, and she received what was called the Baptism of the Holy Ghost. She felt the fire of God and spoke in other tongues. Nothing like this was ever even mentioned in the Methodist Church. Her life was changed forever. Buck and Brad also received the baptism, and began to witness throughout Cedar Falls. A new family came forth, all united in ONE, the person of the Lord Jesus Christ. Hearts were healed, sins were forgiven, life was restored from the dead, and this family began to change multitudes around them. Even the country club crowd who first ran from them began to come around and inquire about this Jesus. Life was GOOD!

2

RELIGION

Jimmy told Ashley he was going out to witness. He had to win some souls or he would perish, or so he told her. Ashley was so proud of her little preacher husband because he had such a heart for the lost. Out the door he scooted. He is so zealous, she thought. Jimmy couldn't wait to get out. He went around the back side of town, came up to Ruby's condo, and knocked on the door.

"I've been waiting on you, she said. "Come in, and make yourself comfortable." After it was over, they rested a minute in the glow of the moment.

Then Jimmy said, "I've got to witness to somebody else."

Ruby laughed. "That's right, go save some more lost souls."

Buck had been talking it over with Susie, and they had decided to start going to Pastor Jimmy Hawkins' little home fellowship. They felt that they had gotten more out of that in the last few weeks than they had at the Methodist Church in the last 19 years. Buck had to go through town to get to Jimmy's home. As Buck walked down the brick sidewalks of downtown Cedar Falls, he couldn't help but notice the stores that had closed. There were more than he could remember. There had not been much to attract outside businesses until the oil boom. Because of the new oil and gas boom, some stores were being remodeled getting ready for the influx of business. There was one part of town that still had a cobblestone street for about a block. He thought how rustic and quaint that was. He wished the whole of Main Street was made of cobble stone. As he got to the end of the cobble stone, he saw Ruby's condo. Coming from around the back of the building was none other than Pastor Jimmy Hawkins.

"Hey!" said Buck. "Wass up?"

Jimmy, knowing he had been caught said, "I been out witnessing trying to get some converts."

Buck knew that was a lie. Jimmy was always dressed to the nines and every thing was in place, but this time his shirt tail was hanging out of his trousers. "Witnessing, huh?"

"Yep, but I got to go. Ashley is waiting lunch on me."

Immediately a dark figure ran behind Ruby's condo. That was strange, thought Buck.

Buck was confused. He had been to Ruby's many times, but since his conversion, he was no longer interested in that. Why would this spiritual man make a trip to Ruby's house? He knew it was not for witnessing. He did remember that Jimmy had witnessed to him about his lust. Takes one to know one, he thought. He was resolved to confront him about that the next time he saw him. But, for now his picture of the perfect spiritual man was crushed.

Buck's main mission today was to go see Pastor Goodman. He had to tell him of his conversion and that he would no longer be going to the Methodist Church. It was the least he could do since he had been going there so many years and because he was a good tither. He thought his income to the church might be missed. As he walked up the steps to the church, he noticed the size of the massive double front doors. They were very ornate. He also noticed the windows, each one having a beautifully colored relief of some saint doing something spiritual. He pushed the doors open, walked through the entry foyer, down the aisle and out the back door past the baptistery. Mayor Tom Berkely was coming down the hall. "Good morning, Buck."

"Good morning, Mayor. What's up with you today?

"Well, I just came to see Pastor Goodman. With all the new people coming into town because of the oil and gas boom, some of them were looking for a good traditional church to get associated with. Since I have been an elder here for quite some time now, I thought I would give our good pastor a list of names that he could call on."

"Interesting. I guess it's a good idea to get them early before our baptist and Pentecostal friends snap them up."

"Yep! Good day, Buck."

"Good day, Mayor."

Walking down the hall, Buck noticed no one was in their office or walking around or taking a break. It seemed vacant except for his encounter with the Mayor. He came to the pastor's office and eased the door open ever so quietly. His eyes bugged out. There was Pastor Goodman on his knees next to the now open closet apparently praying. In front of him was a pedestal with a miniature totem pole on it. At the top of the pole was the same dark figure he saw on the Catholic Church. It looked like a Gargoyle with its wings spread ready to fly. Next to it was that knife he had previously on his desk. Pastor Goodman was making some kind of incantations toward it, and was very fervent in his prayer.

Buck said, "Excuse me, Pastor Goodman."

Immediately Pastor Goodman shot up to a standing position. "Ahem," he said. I was just straightening out my closet. Buck knew that was a lie. One morning, two ministers, two lies. What is going on? he thought. "Pastor Goodman, do you have a minute to talk to me?

"Well, I was on my break, but I guess so. Come in," he angrily replied as he put the pedestal and the totem and the knife back in the closet and locked it. "What can I help you with?"

"Pastor, my wife and I have had a very enlightening experience with God since Brad's wreck. We have been saved and filled with the Holy Ghost. I just wanted to come by and let you know that I appreciate all the spiritual guidance you have given us over the years, but that we are resigning from our affiliation with the church. I hope that doesn't hurt your feelings or anything for it is nothing personal. We are just going on."

"You know, Buck, you were saved when you claimed and enrolled in membership here at this church. I can't be responsible for your soul if you leave. In fact, you may well lose your salvation. I just want you to know the gravity of your choice to move on. Do you really think it is the right thing to do since it may put your soul in jeopardy?"

"Pastor, I wasn't really expecting that reply, but, yes, it is the right decision. My soul is now in God's hands, thank you." With that, Buck gets up and starts for the door and abruptly turns, "Pastor, I clearly saw you praying to that totem pole. I won't forget that." About the time he was ready to leave, he noticed a dark object behind the pastor's desk like before, but this time, it seemed to pause and sneer at him. And then disappeared as before through the bookshelves. Buck rushed out the door to go tell Susie of the most recent events.

When Buck got home, he couldn't wait to talk to Susie. She was out on their covered patio reading a book entitled, "He Came To Set The Captives Free", by Rebecca Brown.

"What ya' reading, babe? He asked.

"It is an enlightening book about people being bound up by their sins, and Jesus sets them free," she said.

"Sounds perfect, because I have some people that are bound by the devil and they definitely need to get set free."

"What are you talking about? Susie asked.

"Susie, this town is bound up beyond belief. And there is a major dominating demon taking everybody down. You remember that Gargoyle I saw over the Catholic Church?"

"Yes!"

"Well, I saw it again. When I went to Pastor Goodman's office, he was kneeling down praying to a totem pole with a Gargoyle on top of it.

"What? That is impossible. He is a pastor."

"I don't know what to tell you, but I saw what I saw. I told him we would not be coming back to the church, and he told me my soul would be in jeopardy....Which, of course, I don't believe. When I was leaving his office, I saw that same black spirit behind his desk. Only this time, he stopped and sneered at me."

"Buck, I don't know what to say. Pastor Goodman is an excellent man. Surely, all this is not true."

"I don't know what to think about any of this. Also, the Mayor was leaving his office rather hurriedly. Of course, he is always busy and got a lot of appointments everyday. And I don't remember seeing a list of names on the Pastor's desk he was talking about. Guess he could have put it in his drawer or his pocket. But, you haven't heard it all yet."

"There's more?"

"Yep! I had to walk by Ruby's condo and who should I see walking out the back door. None other than Pastor Jimmy. He said he was witnessing, but he was rather, uhhhh, disheveled to say the least, and he appeared quite embarrassed. What do you think about that?"

"It's all so unbelievable! After reading some of this book, I now realize that the flesh is weak. We have to do something about all this." That night, Buck and Susie prayed, "Lord, help us to help others."

The next day, Buck started out for Jimmy's house. He reasoned if he could get Jimmy lined out, he would have a powerful ally to conquer the other strongholds. As he got within a block of Jimmy's house, he started to back out. What if he rejects me? What if he gets angry with me? What if his wife finds out? All these things raced through his mind and more. Never-the-less, he knew in his heart of hearts he had to go on. He knocked on his door and Ashley opened and was there to meet him. He could tell she had been crying. Her face was red, her cheeks puffy, and her eyes were bloodshot and had dark bags underneath. Buck started to leave when she said, "Please come in, Buck."

Jimmy came out of the bedroom. He had been crying, too. "Come in, Buck, and have a seat." Before Buck could speak, Jimmy started to confess. "Buck, I have had a terrible problem with pornography all my life. I thought I could hide it, but it began to consume me, and then I began to act it out. I wasn't witnessing yesterday when you found me. I was at Ruby's."

"I know," said Buck. "I just want you to know that you helped me break the spirit of lust, and I wanted to help you. It's all between me and you and God."

"I confessed all my infidelities to Ashley this morning. I knew I had been caught, and that I needed to get right. Ruby was not the only one I had been having sex with. Of course, she was appalled, incensed, angry, and felt rejected. I think after I confessed though that after all the emotions have flowed through her we can still make it. She forgave me for everything. I could hardly believe it. It has been a rough night and morning, but I do believe daylight and a new life are up ahead. Thank you so much for checking on me.'

RELIGION

"OK!" I really didn't know all this was going to be so easy."

"So you will know, it has not been easy for us."

"I know and I understand. Look, I really didn't do anything, but the Holy Ghost has. I'm going to let y'all rest and reconcile for about a week, but I have some serious issues to face, and I know you can help me."

"Of course, whatever you need."

"I'll get back in a week and see how you are doing. Then we can make a battle plan to destroy this kingdom of darkness over Cedar Falls. OK?"

"OK," said Jimmy.

Brad was furious when he found out about Jimmy. "I'm going to get Amy to quit going there," he told his Mom.

"You will do no such thing," she quipped. Your Dad has already talked to him and he has repented and made everything right with his wife. He is going to give a testimony about God's deliverance this Wednesday night. You might do well to be there and see true humility at work."

"Hmmmmm, yes ma'am!"

Pastor Goodman was filling out his resignation papers. He had already accepted a homosexual church in San Francisco which he was eager to serve in. In fact, the associate there was looking for a new intimate friend. He had a picture of him on the church's web page, and he was really cute he thought. At least, out there, folks would understand him with his sexual leanings and his spiritual yearnings toward the dark side. They were more liberal out there and not so accusatory or condemnatory. Clearly, he knew his time was over here in Cedar Falls, what with Buck walking in on him in his moment of reverence to his god. There would be no explaining that to his congregation. They would never understand his deep revelations of the dark side that gave him much pleasure. His members had all been attending over 30 years, and were dead as a hammer today as they were back then....And dumb as a rock. His plane left early the next morning, and he couldn't wait to get on it. No need to resign with a thirty day notice. It would just prolong the agony, and he would be subjected to an obtuse number of questions he was not willing to answer for these nitwits. He quickly threw all the contents of his desk in a cardboard box. Since he was in such a rush to get home and pack, it never occurred to him to clean his closet out at all.

Wednesday night finally arrived. Many had heard about Pastor Jimmy, but didn't know exactly what it was that he did. However, lurid minds want to know about the evil lurking within. Jimmy and Ashley's home was packed out. As far as they could remember, they never had a crowd like this. Their home was wall to wall people in the living room and spilling over into the kitchen. It must have been 50 people crowded in that small home. It was not so much that all those attending were so interested in worshipping as they were to find out all the sordid details about Jimmy's transgression, whatever that was. Surprisingly, Ashley was beaming and singing to the top of her voice, Jimmy was playing the guitar, and the song "Amazing Grace" flooded the room. Even the gawkers and curiosity seekers couldn't help but sing as the room was filled with the spirit. Buck and Susie, and Brad and Amy were right in front singing to the top of their voice with hands raised to heaven. After about 30 minutes of high praise and worship, the music stopped and Jimmy stood up. He picked up his Bible and said, "Would you open the word to Isaiah 53 versus 3 through 6."

Someone in the back of the room hollered out, "We didn't come here to get a lesson today. We came to hear about what it was you did, and what you are going to do about it."

Another hollered out as well, "Yeah!"

And then another, "Tell us everything so we can decide what we need to do with you."

It was like the demons of hell showed up. Jimmy felt like the Sanhedrin had showed up and his life was on trial for his transgressions. And, perhaps it was. Jimmy knew whatever went on here today could mean the end of his and Ashley's ministry in Cedar Falls. Some of these people obviously were out for blood. The most outspoken had rarely come to the meetings, never supported the ministry, usually showed up late and left early, and always stayed in the back. They definitely were not committed to the work, but for some reason they seemed to be really vocal now as if they had a voice in the overthrow of Jimmy and Ashley.

Suddenly, Buck spoke up. "Brothers and sisters, you all know how that a short time ago, God saved me, changed my family and filled us all with the Holy Ghost. Our lives have been forever touched by His presence. Now, we are here to listen to a testimony of a broken man who succumbed to his own lust, but who has already repented. This is supposed to be a testimony to the goodness and mercy of God, and you have not even given him space to speak. I know most of you, especially those of you who are so adamant about hearing all the so called dark details of Jimmy's transgression. In fact, I was there in those moments when you were all in some kind of sin or other. I never saw or heard of you repenting, yet you are here apparently to pass judgment on this righteous man."

"He's not righteous, he's a sinner," someone said in the back.

"He may have committed a sin, but he is the righteousness of God, and one who is redeemed by Christ's blood. If any of you are perfect and without sin, please stand up and declare your holiness before us all. Let us decide if you are worthy to judge this man. Slowly, one of the oldest and most outspoken rose up, hunched over trying to make himself invisible, and walked out the door pulling it to so softly so as not to make a spectacle of his leaving. About 27 in total also left, which oddly enough was exactly the number in the original Sanhedrin in Christ's day. The room was quiet.

Jimmy continued, "Thank you, Buck. And those of you who are left, thank you for your support. God has come to me and forgiven a most heinous transgression for which I am eternally grateful. He has sent something like a refining fire and purged me. My wife, Ashley has totally forgiven me. Our marriage is reconciled. Sometimes sin lurks in the flesh, and only comes out at the greatest moment of temptation. We all are weak in that way. I want to say, if you have a weakness, let us all pray for you, not to gossip, but to sincerely pray you are delivered before you fall so hard like I have. You can be sure, if you have sin or sins, you will be found out. It is just a matter of time. Hands shot up everywhere for those still there.

"Pray for me," they all said. Suddenly, folks were repenting, crying, snotting, confessing, and laying their sins bare. An awesome spiritual moment was happening in Cedar Falls. Sins were being forgiven, and the spirit of religion was being broken. Those that stayed were set free. Those that had left had a new respect for grace. They knew they would never sit on another board of the Sanhedrin of the 21st century. In fact, they knew they would never judge a man before they heard all the facts. In fact, they knew they would not judge anyone from that time forward.

News of the meeting spread like wildfire. Father Bordelon of the Catholic Church heard all about it. Some of the outspoken critics at the charismatic meeting were actually members of his church. He had always been one quick to judge. He was hard against abortion, didn't like protestants or anyone so called outside of the universal church. Being a very religious man, he felt he was justified to condemn all outside the faith. He heard many confessions in the last 10 years since his transfer here, and he knew the sins of much of the towns folk in Cedar Falls, not because they all came to confess, but that those that came to confess told all about them. He had an obligation to keep confidentiality with everyone as a man of the cloth. His transfer here was not what he wanted, because he had higher aspirations to go to a bigger parish. But, this was not a promotion. Some kids, no, stupid altar boys had told on him and how he fondled them. He had mutual masturbation with one 14 year old on a regular basis. As far as he knew, he didn't tell on him. The altar boys in Cedar Falls giggled when he played with their penises. He felt like they would not tell. His next assignment was right around the corner, and he yearned for the day he could get out of this hick cowboy town. There was one problem, Bobby Blaxton.

Bobby Blaxton was the town tramp and alcoholic. He had been to see Father Bordelon several times. Bobby, in his alcoholic state could go either way. He was bisexual. His sins seemed to be ever before him. Never could he break the hold of sin on his life. He couldn't quit drinking, he couldn't quit cussin', he couldn't quit smokin', he couldn't quit having sex whether it was male or female. Even some of the most respectable women would come to him because he was known for his bizarre sex acts. Father Bordelon had confession with him a few times. On finding out that Bobby had homosexual tendencies at one confessional, he invited Bobby to his office for a pep-me-up drink. Bobby was really down that day. As he entered the Father's office, he was instructed to sit down on the big leather couch on the side of the room. Father Bordelon sat right beside him. They sipped on their drinks that the Father poured, and talked about nonsensical

RELIGION

things. Shortly, Father Bordelon put his hand on Bobby's knee. Bobby had no resistance.

After it was over, Bobby said, "Well, that's all I got time for today, Father. Maybe I can help you next time. Got to go." Bobby quickly moved out the door. Never in all my life have I done anything like that, he thought. That was a minister, a clergyman, a man of the cloth. Not sure if he had committed a cardinal sin, he began to hurry home to contemplate what just happened. For once in his life, he felt conviction about what went down. It didn't seem right to do that with one of God's chosen. As he walked out of the church, he heard a flutter above him. A monstrous looking creature was on top of the bell tower with his wings outstretched and flapping. An eerie feeling came over Bobby and he ran, yes he ran real fast to his home. He knew he had messed up this time.

"Brrring," the phone rang and Buck answered. It was Bobby Blaxton.

"Buck, look this is Bobby Blaxton. I think I've got real trouble with God now. I have heard about what happened to you and Brad and Amy and all that hoopla over at Jimbo's church."

"You mean Pastor Jimmy?"

"Yeah, Jimmy. I have called him Jimbo for so long kinda making fun of his Pentecostal ways, you know speaking in tongues and spiritual gifts and all that stuff. I guess Jimbo stuck. Anyway, I need some help. I may have committed the ultimate cardinal sin. I'm not sure I can be forgiven, not that I have ever tried to in the past, but this time, I think I went too far. What's the chances I could talk to you in person about that?"

"How about I bring Pastor Jimmy along as well. He has been doing this for way longer than me, and he has a lot of wisdom."

"Ok, bring Jimbo. I'm going to be at my apartment."

"Great, let me get a hold of Pastor Jimmy and we will see you, say in 30 minutes?"

"Awesome, the sooner the better."

Buck called Pastor Jimmy to arrange the meeting. He answered after the first ring. "Praise the Lord!" Jimmy exclaimed.

"Boy, you sound like you are on top of the world, said Buck.

"I am! What's not to being on top of the world when your sins are forgiven, your wife loves you, and you are at peace with God."

"Ok! Look, I'm not trying to get you back into warfare what with all that has gone on in the last week…"

"That's alright, I'm ready. Wass up?"

"You remember Bobby Blaxton, the town drunk?"

"I do. What about him?"

"He called me a few minutes ago and needs some help and counsel. I'm still new at all this, so I asked him if I could bring you, if that is alright?"

"Of course, let's go."

Buck picked up Pastor Jimmy and they set out on their new mission…to rescue a lost soul, namely Bobby Blaxton. As they drove up to his apartment, they noticed it was in a state of disrepair and the grass needed mowing. They knocked on the door. "Come in, the door is open," came the response from within.

"Hey, Bobby."

"Hey, Buck."

"This is Pastor Jimmy. Jimmy, this is Bobby."

"Nice to meet you, Bobby."

Bobby had them sit down. They had to throw old newspapers out of the way, move the take out box of ribs, and make a place to sit. They noticed dishes were in the sink, and the place looked like it had not been vacuumed or cleaned in like forever. It smelled really bad of second hand smoke which made Jimmy almost gag. The smoke burned his eyes and for a moment everything got blurry. He was just not used to this kind of environment. The sinners were not in the church, he remembered. They were in the world, and right now, the world was calling for help.

Bobby began to speak. "I don't know how to tell you guys this, but I think I have really messed up."

"What do you mean?" Jimmy asked.

"Well, I have committed a lot of sins. I get drunk all the time, I cuss, I smoke, I've done some dope from time to time, and I run around with a lot of loose women, some trashy and some classy. I've even been known to cross over the heterosexual world from time to time when I was real drunk. If you know what I mean. Now, I will tell you, I'm not real proud of my life. And I don't know why God has let me live this long, but He may not after today."

"What do you mean? Buck said.

"I mean, I just had sex with a minister, and I don't mean a woman minister, I mean a man of the cloth. You can't imagine how bad I feel. Never in my life have I felt so ashamed. At any moment, I could throw up. I am disgusted with myself."

"What happened, Bobby? We don't need to know all the sordid details, but in a nutshell, what happened?"

"You know Father Bordelon at the Catholic Church, right?"

"We do."

"After confessional...I go there from time to time to unload...you know what I mean. Well, this last time which was today, he invited me to his office after confessional. I sat down on his couch, drank a little wine with him, and he put his hand on my leg. You know what I'm talking about when I say put his hand on me, right?"

"We do."

Anyway, he quickly began to do his thing. I'm afraid I let him, he finished and I hurried out the church. I was really feeling bad I made a man of the cloth fall like that. But, that wasn't all. As I got outside, I saw a huge ugly creature with his wings spread on top of the bell tower. That wasn't the death angel, was it? I'm really afraid I don't have long left to live."

"Whoa, slow down Bobby. Said Pastor Jimmy. All is going to be alright."

"Are you sure? I don't want to die right now. I'm only 40 years old."

"For starters, Bobby, you haven't committed the unpardonable sin. Secondly, you are not going to die. Thirdly, you are going to live, and you will live to a ripe old age."

"How do you know all that, Pastor?"

"It's all written in his word!" Jimmy proudly proclaimed. "Look, Bobby, you have not done anything that any one of is not capable or has not already done. Jesus is there for you just like he was there for us. He paid for your sins on the cross and his blood washes them away when you call out to him. How would you like to receive him as your savior, right now?"

"Man, I'm ready! This is all a heavy load on me. I can hardly bear it. What have I got to do?"

"Just ask him into your heart."

"That's it? Just ask him into my heart? It sounds too easy. I don't have to live right for a while, then do it?"

"Nope, he takes you just like you are."

"Ok! Well, here goes. Jesus, come into my heart! Whoa! What was that?"

"What do you mean?" Inquired Buck.

"I felt something! Man, I mean I really felt something. It feels like somebody is taking a scouring pad and washing me out on the inside. I feel clean. WOW! I mean I feel really clean! Thank you, Jesus! Thank you, Jesus! Thank you, Jesus! This is awesome. Is this what happened to ya'll?" Bobby asked.

"It is, Bobby. Your new life has started right now. God has saved you and delivered you in one fell swoop."

"What do you mean He has delivered me? Bobby asked.

"I mean you probably don't want to drink, smoke, sin, run around with women, or have any other perversions in your life. You are free."

"Glory to God," said Bobby. "I'm free. I'm saved. I'm delivered. I'm a new man. And all the above and more. Never have I ever felt like this. How come you guys never told me about this before now?"

"You weren't ready before now," Buck explained. Your sins had to come to the full and your repentance had to be real. Finally, you were fed up with your life, and really wanted to change. God met you there."

"Well, all I can say is "Thank you, Jesus" for all you have done for me. This is by far the greatest thing to ever happen to me. Thank you, guys for coming to my rescue, also. If y'all had not come, I wouldn't have known what to do."

Buck and Jimmy left Bobby's apartment feeling really good about what the Lord had done through them. At the moment, they were on a spiritual high just like Bobby. Jimmy went home and Buck went to see Father Bordelon.

"Father Bordelon, my name is Buck Merriman."

"Hi, Buck, what can I help you with today? Do you need to go to confessional, or do you need to do some "Hail Mary's", or do you need

RELIGION

some prayer beads? I have never seen you around here before. Do you want to become a Catholic?"

"Actually, none of the above. I have come to talk to you about Bobby Blaxton."

"Oh, yes, poor ole' Bobby. He is a drunk you know, and sometimes quite delusional. You can't depend on anything he says."

"Hold on, I need to talk to you about what went on in your office today."

"Well, he came to my office all right, and said he had some sins to confess, and I had him do seven "Hail Mary's", and he left."

"Father, don't you usually take confessions in the confession booth, and not in your office? Plus, Bobby's recounting of the incidents of today do not line up with yours."

"Like I said, he is a drunk and so many times he is quite delusional just as he was today. Is that all I can help you with?"

"Let me be clear. Bobby said he was in your office today and that you went down on him."

"Down on him? Oh, no, I never pray to a man nor do I let one pray to me."

"Father Bordelon, you are not getting my message. Let me be even more clear. Bobby said you performed oral sex on him. Is that true?"

"You need to get out of here. You are so disrespectful to my high office. And the lies and innuendos that drunk said about me is totally off the charts. I'll not be maligned by your insinuations. This meeting is over."

Buck left the church thinking, That didn't go like I planned. But, he didn't have time to reflect on it that much for when he got into the sunlight, he heard the rush of wings above. There was that creature lifting off of the bell tower. This time he thought he heard as it were, a raucous laughter as he flew away.

Samuel Trace, Pastor of First Baptist was walking down Main Street when he ran into Buck. Sam, as his friends called him was nervous as a cat on the proverbial hot tin roof. "Buckkkk," he stammered. I can't help but tell you that you are getting quite the reputation around here as some kind of spiritual Wyatt Earp. Seems like you and Jimmy down there at the charismatic home group have been cleaning house.

I really don't want you at my church. Do you understand? There is no need for any of that so called glossalia, either."

"I do, Pastor Sam," Buck said very respectfully. "Let me ask you, do you have something to hide?"

"Whyyy, Whyy, Why would you ask that question?"

"You talk and seem like you just got caught with your hand in the cookie jar, that's why."

"I haven't, but..."

"Uh, Oh, somebody has. You know, Pastor, God knows all our secret sins, and he is gracious and merciful to forgive us if we confess them. If there is something going on, know for sure you will be found out."

"Buck, I need to talk to you in private. Would you come to my office in about an hour?"

"Sure," See you then.

An hour later, Buck is walking in Pastor Sam's office at the First Baptist Church. It was not as elaborate as Pastor Goodman's office, but he did have a small library on the side, a nice brown office desk and chair and two straight back chairs in front of his desk. "Have a seat, Buck. And, thank you for coming."

"Sure thing," Buck replied.

"Buck, you know things have been hard around here with the agricultural bust. Farmers are going out of business right and left, and make up the majority of my church. This new oil boom has brought in a lot of new people, but they are not interested in our church. Our tithes and offerings have fallen off drastically. Me and my wife's income was based on a modest salary of $25,000 per year plus 10% of offerings above a certain amount. These have fallen off almost altogether."

"Why are you telling me all this? Buck asked.

"I'm getting to that. My wife, Julie is the secretary-treasurer of the church, and I emphasize treasurer. She handles all the money and nobody sees to her hand. The reason I'm telling you this is that I think she is stealing from the church."

"How would you know that?"

"The income in the church has gone down, but our personal income has not. In fact, it has grown, and quite considerably I might add. I'm sick over it, but I just don't know what to do. We have been having marital problems for a couple of years, and we have lost all communication.

RELIGION

I simply am at the point I just don't know what to do. It's on the street that you and Pastor Jimmy have been cleaning house, you are very well to do, and you are well respected in the community. I want to know if you can help me. I don't want anything to happen to my wife for I love her, even though she may not reciprocate. I'm really lost at sea in an open ocean right now."

"Pastor, it seems like I read where a man is guilty of his own sins. I suggest you call the regional council of churches for the Baptist association here and have them come in and do an audit. I think, first you need to be sure there is an impropriety. Your wife may have income you know not of."

"Of course, that is a great idea. I will do that first thing in the morning. Thank you for your time, Buck."

Bishop Barry Ebert, pastor of the United Pentecostal Church in town was in his office one Saturday morning getting ready for his Sunday sermon. The door flew open and in walked Sister Anne, the wife of Elder Tom. Tom was one of the major contributors of the church since the oil boom for he had land that he leased to the oil companies, and he was making a lot of money every month from those leases. His time had come. Sister Anne had on a long sleeved dress with a floor length hem. Her hair was in a bun, and she had no makeup on. She was straight line Pentecost. It really made no difference for she was one drop dead gorgeous woman with or without makeup. She sashshed right behind Bishop Barry's desk, and said, "I need some prayer."

Barry knew exactly what that meant. After the encounter, Sister Anne said, "Ok, thanks for the prayer." And off she went.

Bishop Barry was used to these quickies for there were several of the ladies in the church that were willing to do God a favor by having sex with him. It was the perverted teaching of the "vestal virgins" that did it. They were to remain chaste with men, but they could have sex with a holy leader, and did not lose their chastity. It was taught in such a way, only the enlightened ones could understand it. Once they got it, they came to him with wild abandon. There was a handful of them, no make that a double handful, he revered. No one ever knew.

Pastor Jimmy was praying that afternoon, "Lord, help us to root out, tear down and build up." About that same time, he had a vision. He saw an ancient priest stretch out his rod of authority. Blood was dripping off the end of it. He stretched it out to two people. On the forehead of one, the word was written, repentant; on the forehead of the other was the word reprobate. When the rod touched the one that had the word repentant, a bright light appeared. When it touched the one that had reprobate on his head, darkness blotted him out. Jimmy was extremely startled by the vision. What did that mean, he thought. And then the word came, "GO TO BISHOP BARRY."

Jimmy was shocked. He didn't know Bishop Barry very well though he had talked with him at some ecumenical pastor's meetings from time to time. Really, he had no relationship with him. What was he to say? Or was he just to listen? The Lord was silent.

Joe had finished his work at the clubhouse, repaired several houses that had been ripped up by the storm, and was walking down Main Street when he saw Bishop Barry walking toward him. Joe stopped on the corner, and waited for Barry to pass by. As soon as Barry got to the corner, he said his typical hello to Joe. Here was another yokel come to town he thought. Joe caught his eyes. Barry felt like he was hit by a fire. Joe's eyes seemed to scatter sin wherever he looked. Barry was feeling really unclean. Who is this guy?, he pondered. Like a welder's torch, a fire lit up in Barry's belly. It raced through his body burning out the dross. "My, God," Barry said as he grabbed the light post to keep from falling. Jimmy walked up at the same time. Joe turned and left. Jimmy reached out to Barry to hold him up.
"You are just the man I want to see," Jimmy said.
Barry was speechless. "About what," he questioned.
"I'm not sure, but I had a vision a while ago and the Lord specifically told me to come see you." In the next few minutes, Jimmy expounded the vision he had gotten earlier to Barry. "What do you think that vision means, Bishop Barry?"
"I'm pretty sure I know, Barry said. "It was directed toward me. Barry had been really feeling recalcitrant until he met Joe, but right now he was really feeling repentant. "Jimmy, I don't know what has just happened to me, but I'm a changed man as of just a few minutes ago."
"What happened?"

RELIGION

"I was just going along here minding my own business, when that new man in town, you know the carpenter named Joe walked by. He just looked at me, and a fire built up in my belly and swept through my body. I haven't exactly been sin free, but for some reason, I know I'm really clean, and free from sin. You know what I mean?"

"I know exactly what you mean. Something similar has happened to me and ole' Buck Merriman within the last week. Buck was at the country club when he ran into that guy, and he came away a new man. I don't know who he is, but he is sure making the rounds."

Bishop Barry left Jimmy and went straight back to the church. His secretary was leaving for the day. "What are you doing here, Bishop? I thought you were gone for the day."

"Got to redo my sermon," he said. He pulled out a clean sheet of paper and wrote across the top, "Forgiveness to Live Holy."

Close to the end of the following week, the overseers of the regional Baptists came to visit First Baptist Church to do an audit. Sam had told his wife Julie about the audit, but never mentioned a word that she might be a suspect. The audit took a full day, but it looked like over $100,000 had been misappropriated. Julie had been pacing the floor like an expectant parent all day. Her clothes were soaking wet when Sam came up to her. "Julie," the regional board wants to talk to you. Can you go in and see them?"

"About what," she quipped.

"It appears there is a little over $100,000 missing from the church coffers. They want to know if you know anything about it that might help them.

"How do you think we have been able to maintain our standard of living? Do you think money just appears on trees? I have worked hard for this family and I will not be brought into question about anything. If it weren't for me, you, my poor pitiful husband would be out on the street."

"What? You mean you took that money?"

"Of course, I did, you idiot. This bunch of bumpkins will never miss it, and besides, we deserve it."

Sam began to weep, "Julie, Julie, Julie! Why, oh why, oh why?"

"Shut up, you ungrateful wretch. You have put that holier than thou and religious attitude on me for the last time. Get out of my sight. I can't stand to look at you."

Sam was now horrified. All these years, he had dedicated himself to serving the Lord, and now it looked like those years of service had been for naught. He reluctantly went in and told the board what he just found out.

"We have no choice," said the board. "Hopefully, she would have been more repentant, but now it looks like we are going to have to do something we even detest. Somebody go call Sheriff Kelly Vargas."

Sheriff Vargas listened quietly as the board's spokesman reiterated the day's findings. "I'm afraid we have no choice but to file charges against the Pastor's wife. We don't want to do it, but according to him, she is not remorseful at all."

"I understand, " Kelly said. This is going to be a hard day for me for sure. Kelly went reluctantly to Sam's house and knocked on the door. Julie opened it and was shocked to see Sheriff Kelly Vargas standing there.

"What do you need? Sheriff?" Sarcastically.

"Going somewhere, Julie? You seem to be packing your bags."

"I'm getting out of Dodge," she spat.

"Oh, I don't think so. You have the right to remain silent. Anything you say can and will be used against you in a court of law. You have the right to speak to an attorney, and to have an attorney present during any questioning. If you cannot afford a lawyer, one will be provided for you at government expense. Turn around. I'm sorry, Julie, but I have to put these cuffs on you."

"You SOB, you know this ain't right. They owe me."

"Whether it's right or not, I don't know. It's up to a court of law to determine that. You know I am one of the best members of your and Sam's church, and me and my wife have been faithful tithers for years. It doesn't set well with me that money you have charge over has been misappropriated. Of course, that ain't the reason I'm here. Although, it does put a bad taste in my mouth. And another thing, I didn't know you could cuss, and so you will know I don't like being cussed. Get in the car, Julie."

On the way to the station, Julie let out another string of profanities like he had never heard one person say, not even in the four years he had been in the Marine Corps.

Pastor Sam met the sheriff at his office as soon as he brought Julie in. "Sheriff, can I bail her out?"

"We just got here and I haven't had a judge set bail yet, Pastor. I am so sorry. Afraid she is going to spend a few days in jail though. I wish I could let her go of her own recognizance, but she is considered a flight risk since I found her packing to leave."

"What? Packing to leave?"

"Yep, she was checking out."

"I am sick, I mean I am really sick."

"Pastor, after what she has done and what I heard come out of her mouth, this is not the first time you have ever had problems with her, right?"

Sam sheepishly lowered his head. "Nope, we have been married for 15 years and it all started on our wedding night. I have been able to hide it all these years till now. I was so hopeful she would get saved, but it never happened. Our marriage has been seriously on the rocks for the last 2 years. I guess today splits the sheets for good. My only regret, really, is that I will lose this church. The people are wonderful, and I have enjoyed serving here. I think there has been a lot of good come out of my tenure."

"Oh, I think once everything is explained to the board, you may find out things are not as bad off as it may now seem."

Father Bordelon had already lost one good parish, only to be demoted to this "hell hole". He was not going to be demoted again. He felt like he did justice to his services. Many even said he conducted the best Mass they had ever attended. He knew Latin better than 90 % of other priests, and he had raised up the best altar boys one could find anywhere. They satisfied all the Father's spiritual and physical needs. Once Buck found out about his encounter with Bobby though, he knew it was only time, yes even a short time till it hit the fan or so he thought. Sitting at his desk and contemplating the days's events, Father Bordelon opened the bottom drawer where his 22 LR Rimfire–Smith & Wesson was located. He put the gun on his desk, checked it for cartridges, and pulled the safety off. He sat there for an hour just staring at it. This would be a good day to relieve some stress, he mused. Instead of strapping a holster to his chest, and sheathing his pistol, he raised it to his head. Blammmm! The huge black ominous creature outside on the bell tower lifted his wings and began to circle the church in a victory swoop. Some of the townsfolk heard his decadent cry. An evil presence fell over Cedar Falls, and the sun got dark for about 15 minutes.

A few days after all the recent events, it occurred to Jimmy that he needed to call an Ecumenical meeting of the local ministers. He called Buck first simply because Buck seemed to be the stimulus that propagated all the drama of late. "Buck, it looks like God is doing a house cleaning. You remember that vision I had with the priest holding the rod with blood dripping off the end?"

"I sure do."

"It appears he is stretching it out to many in this community. Those that repent are reconciled, and those that are hardened are moved out or eliminated. I have never seen anything like this in all my life. We need to get the remaining pastors together to talk about what is going on and figure out the best way to pursue a further course of action."

"Great idea. Let's get busy."

At lunch the next day, Pastor Sam had graciously allowed everyone to meet in his conference room at the First Baptist Church. They had Chinese catered from a local hole in the wall called "Empire". It was run by some Chinese immigrants who had come to Cedar Falls because of the oil and gas boom. Not only was their business good, but their food was outstanding. Those at the meeting were Pastor Jimmy, Pastor Sam, Bishop Barry Ebert, and Buck. Glaringly missing were Pastor Goodman and Father Bordelon.

"I guess y'all know why we have called this meeting," Jimmy said. In the last few weeks, we have experienced spiritual warfare on an unprecedented scale. Pastor Goodman's exodus and Father Bordelon's demise should be a sign to all of us that God is serious about his church. And when I say church, I mean all of the saints in all our churches, not just one. "Can I get a witness?"

"Amen!" They all said in unison. "What do you think we need to do now?" Barry asked.

"Gentleman, we need to fight. Through the grapevine, I heard Pastor Goodman is taking a homosexual Methodist church in California. The Methodist board is sending a replacement here right away. The Catholic diocese is sending a new priest who will be here in a couple of days. I think we need to bring them in the fold immediately, include them in our Ecumenical meetings, and discretely vet them so we will know what their heart is. If judgment begins first at the house of God, as we all know and have experienced in the last couple of weeks, how much more shall we be held accountable as leaders of the church. Also, there is the matter of these evil spirits that have been appearing everywhere. I know we are led away by our own lusts, but these creatures are perverse, and I think we need to take our God given authority over them and run them out of town. As soon as the ministers from the Methodist and Catholic Church come in, we will have a meeting, then we will all join in a time of serious intercessory prayer. If that is alright with you all"?

"You've got my support," Bishop Barry said.

"And ours," they all said.

"Good, I'll get back to each one of you after these replacements come in."

One week later, the new Methodist minister and the new Catholic priest had officially fulfilled their appointments and set up office. Buck told Pastor Jimmy he thought this was a good time to go visit each one of them, and invite them to the next Ecumenical meeting. Buck took off to the Methodist Church and Jimmy went to the Catholic Church to meet the new ministers.

Buck knocked and was greeted with a pleasant "come in" on the other side of the door. Pastor Love was still busy unpacking boxes and setting up his book shelves. Buck looked and noticed the door to the closet was open and the totem was about half way between the closet and the desk. After introductions and a few pleasantries, Buck ventured out and said, "What are you going to do with that?..... testing the new Pastor.

"I don't know. But, I can tell you one thing... it is hideous. I need to get rid of it somehow...like maybe a rummage sale."

"No, sir, we need to burn it to ashes."

"Why do you say that?"

"It has been used as an object of veneration. I'm afraid it attracts spirits and demons," knowing when he said that, the cat was out of the bag so to say, and his radical beliefs were on the table.

"Whoa! You mean someone has been worshipping this thing. For sure then, I think you are right, we will definitely need to destroy it. It was here in the closet. Who in the world would worship it?"

Buck was asked a straight forward question, so he was going to give him a straight forward answer even if it hair lipped the devil. "It was the last Pastor, Pastor Goodman. Do you know him?"

"I don't really know him, but his reputation has preceded him. I think his next assignment was a homosexual church out west somewhere. At least, that is the gossip."

"Yep, he has some really liberal leanings, plus some serious idolatry. I caught him myself bowed down to that thing. We have been getting a lot of demonic sightings around here of late and some weird things have been happening. We might just go right ahead and burn it now if it is ok with you?"

"You bet! The last church I was in was definitely demonically oppressed. I didn't find out until after I left that my main elder and his wife were involved in a witch's cult. They gave me problems from the first day I arrived three years ago. Apparently, many of the elite folks in the city I was in were also in that cult. That elder made a shambles of the church, and brought a railing accusation of infidelity on me. My wife almost left me over it. Of course, it was not true, but you know how accusations are. Once they are made, you have to prove them wrong. It's not like in a court of law where you are innocent until proven guilty. I hate devils. Let's get on with it."

Buck picked up the totem, grabbed some packing paper for kindling, found some matches in a drawer, and the two of them headed out back. There was about 50' of back yard, and then about 100' of trees in a little grove. They didn't want to arouse much interest, so they headed to the little grove of trees. Inside the grove, they found a clearing. Buck kicked back some leaves and lo' and behold, he stirred up some bones.

Most of them were small animal bones, but there was one small foot which looked like a child's foot. It was charred, but it was definitely human. "Looks like we have stirred up some kind of ritual altar," Buck said. We better not burn this thing yet. No need to destroy evidence that might be useful to the authorities." Back to the church they went with the totem, put it back in the closet for now, and locked it.

Buck put in a call to Sheriff Kelly Vargas. "Sheriff, this is Buck, Buck Merriman."

"I know, Buck. I recognize your voice. What's up?"

"Sheriff, that new pastor at the Methodist Church and I were talking and went outside to look at the property that the church was on. We ran into some bones in that little grove of woods behind the church. I think we kicked up a kid's foot." Buck didn't think it was the right time to tell the Sheriff what the real reason the two of them were out there at this time. Maybe later, he thought.

"Oh, my God! What next? Sheriff Vargas said. Be right out, Buck. Don't go anywhere. I will need you to show me right where you were looking."

"Yes, sir! Better bring along forensics while you are at it."

Twenty minutes later, Sheriff Vargas drives up with his lights flashing. Behind him were the other two patrol cars. The forensic expert was right in tow. "Where is the location of those bones, Buck?"

"Follow me."

After Buck showed him the site, Sheriff Vargas wanted him to stand clear of the grove. "This forensic guy needs to gather some evidence for a while. Y'all don't need to stay here. This might take a while."

Buck said, "OK! I'm going to check on Pastor Jimmy. He was supposed to meet with the Catholic pastor today."

The meeting with Father Inzina went as planned. Pastor Jimmy walked right up to the Father's office door which was already open. Father Inzina was busy at his desk when Jimmy walked in. "Ahem," as Jimmy cleared his throat. Inzina looked up, "Come on in. You must be Pastor Hawkins?"

"Yes, Sir."

"Have a seat, my dear brother."

Jimmy was not a little astonished at his warm welcome. He expected the Father to be a little more stoic. Instead, he seemed very sincere and humble.

"What can I help you with, Pastor?"

"Well, I'm not really looking for any help, but maybe a little. I heard you were in town taking over the church and this a little welcoming hello, get acquainted meeting. And maybe you can help in a matter here in the community if you like."

"You have my attention. What is it?"

"Sir, you know how the last priest died through suicide? But, there is something you may not know, and that is his dark side?" Jimmy was questioning instead of informing him.

"I know all about it. I have been briefed by the Bishop of this Diocese and he has informed me of everything."

"Did he tell you about the demonic activity that has been going on around here?"

"Actually, he didn't. But, I am acutely interested. You may not know this, but I taught "Exorcisms" at our Jesuit college in Verona. I am ready to get in the battle."

"Wow! I didn't for sure expect to hear you say that. You may well be the man we've been looking for."

"Buck, this is Sheriff Vargas. You might be interested in this. We dug around in that little site you put us on. It appears there were others buried. The best our forensics guy can do right now is there were apparently four boys between the ages of 9 and 15. It looks like they were all burned in the fire and buried. Appears we have some witch craft sacrificial ceremonies going on around here not to count that they may have all been sodomized. None of them had any signs of penises. We have their skulls, and each one of them have a hole in them like someone drove a knife in them. Couldn't find any kind of weapon like that though in the site."

"I might be able to shed some light on that, Sheriff. There is a locked closet in the Pastor's office. It may have some clues in it that might help your investigation."

"Like what?"

"Well-l-l-l, there is a totem with a Gargoyle on top, and a reddish bone handled knife."

"What-t-t-t the....? Let's get over there and take a look."

Buck and Sheriff Vargas met Pastor Love in his office shortly after their conversation. Pastor Love was most helpful. He opened the closet, pulled out the totem and the knife for the Sheriff to see.

"Afraid I'm going to have to confiscate these for evidence," he told Pastor Love.

"No problem. I really don't want them around here anyway. That totem is hideous, and I don't want it attracting anything into this office."

Sheriff Vargas had brought a black garbage bag for the totem and a smaller evidence bag for the knife. He put on his rubber gloves, and carefully put each one its own bag. "Thank you, Pastor. If you find anything else around here that you think we might need, please call me."

"Will do. You have a blessed day."

Sheriff Vargas and Buck left. Once they got outside, the Sheriff said to Buck, "I've got to get this stuff to forensics. I want to see if that knife fits those wounds on those skulls, and if so, I need some finger prints, especially those of Pastor Goodman. He may have some hard questions to answer."

The following week, as planned, all of the local pastors got together for an ecumenical meeting. The only non minister was Buck. But, he had been there from the beginning and knew all about what was going on in Cedar Falls. Pastor Sam was a gracious host. The meeting started at 10:00 AM, and culminated with a catered fried chicken lunch with all the trimmings. There was not a minister there that did not like fried chicken. What was it about ministers and fried chicken? Sam thought. When the meeting got started, Sam had Buck come forward and talk about the sightings of the Gargoyle, the miraculous healing of Brad and Amy, the suicide of Father Bordelon, and finally the exposure of Pastor John Goodman in witchcraft, homosexuality, and possibly murder. Each one contributed to the discussion which centered mainly around destroying the spirits of darkness and how to go about it. Buck thought it was not just in the family and religion that was affected by evil spirits, but in every sector of life. With that final statement, they prayed, adjourned, and ate some of that fine fried chicken. Each one resolved to find out if there was more people affected and more sectors of society infiltrated by these evil spirits. It appeared to be righteous men at the heads of all the churches, and unity could be a reality amongst the brethren no matter the affiliation. Now that their awareness had been elevated, they could see more clearly, and recognize when and where the serpent was in action, and make a front against the real enemy of the church and raise a standard.

3

EDUCATION

Cedar Falls, as of the last census had over 39,000 people of which there were 14,000 households and 8000 families. It was mostly white being around 94% while the rest were made up of native Americans, black, Asian, and Hispanic.

There were three public universities, two high schools, of which one was a private Christian school, two junior high schools and six elementary schools along with one parochial Catholic School. Most kids who started high school went on to graduate. Although no one knew why, in the last two years, it was noted that average grades from grammar school all the way through high school began to plummet. Heretofore, kids graduated with academic excellence. The students had extra curricular activities such as football, baseball, basketball, soccer, and track. Cedar Falls was a relatively small town, nevertheless, a few graduates went on to play some kind of collegiate sport.

Bob Stodgell was the School Board President, and had lived in Cedar Falls all his life. He had gone to grammar school and high school there, and attended the local college and gotten his master's degree in education. He rose up to his position through the ranks teaching math on a high school level and taught P.E. He was principal at Cedar Falls High School for 10 years, then was elected to the school board as president 8 years ago. Bob noticed scores were dropping over the last few years, and it did not bode well with him since it was on his watch. It was a puzzle as to the why. The schools had been mandated to institute the "No Child Left Behind" policy and teach "Common Core Curriculum" by the federal government. Although, these two changes to education seemed good at first, it just happened to be that from the time they were enacted, scores started to drop. Both were touted to put America on the fast track of world dominance in education. A reasonable person would not even think about these as being the problem since they were supposed to be the answer to modern education.

Nell Risinger was the 5th grade teacher at Cedar Falls Grammar School. It had been a rough year. Her class had been unruly, disobedient, and almost unteachable since school started. She had never had a year like this. As she watched her last student catch the bus to go home, she thought, I need some help or insight. She called Bob. "Bob, this is Nell. You know I never complain and I'm not complaining now, but I need some help. For some reason, this year, I have not been able to get control of my students. Their grades have fallen off from last year, and it is chaos in my room every day. As far as I know, I'm not doing anything different from what I did last year except try harder. I don't seem to be making an impact on them. You've taught before. Got any ideas?"

"Tell me, Nell. What is different from what you used to do?"

"Well, in the last couple of years, I've noticed kids don't seem to be interested in school like they used to be. They don't score as well on their tests, absolutely refuse to do their homework, and are not attentive in class."

"What's changed in the last couple of years that you can put your finger on?"

"Bob, the only thing I know is the "No Child Left Behind" and the "Common Core Curriculum"."

"Is there a downside to either one of those?"

Nell was hesitant to answer. She knew of teachers in other school districts who lost their jobs because they complained about these particular changes. "Bob, I'm not saying "No Child Left Behind' is a bad policy, but kids are being socially promoted without mastering their school work. It takes the incentive out of them to study. As far as "Common Core" is concerned, it is not the three "R's". Whoever designed this curriculum made something complicated for no reason

EDUCATION

at all. I can see how it is supposed to be dumbed down to let all kids get through school, but it has taken simple principles and confused the issue. In addition, the curriculum is written to totally change American History as we know it. It is real strong on teaching how blacks founded America, the influence Muslims had on developing our culture, it has hard racial overtones, and teaches homosexuality as a preferred lifestyle. I personally don't like it, and I hate teaching it. It's defeating the purpose of education. Leap Tests at the end of the year to see if children are academically qualified to go to the next grade is a farce. We have to take a full month to help them prepare for the test, and it has nothing to do with what they studied during the year. Kids don't even have to study all year, cram for the Leap and they go on to the next grade. Not all kids learn at the same level. The smart ones become bored and unmotivated, the slower ones can't master the material before moving to the next grade and become discouraged. We are graduating dumbed down kids no matter how you look at it. I've perused some of these Christian curriculums, and they absolutely know how to motivate their students no matter what level they are at. And they all excel. Just because you are a certain age doesn't mean that is the grade level you function at. I can't help but think the devil is in the details. Pardon the expression!"

"Nell, I share your frustration, but I must have proof that this you said is the problem. I can't approach this with just your opinion."

"I understand, but it may be difficult to get others to look objectively at this, since any type of criticism may get them fired as has happened in other counties and states. They just put their heads down and teach it whether they like it or not. It is mandated. Of course, you understand their fear, right?"

"I do, Nell, but...."

"And one more thing while I'm at it. I hate these sex education pamphlets. They don't just have the printed word, they have real people engaged in intercourse and homosexual acts. For God's sake, this is the 5th grade and I have to teach kids...got that! Kids... how to have sex, how to use a condom, accept homosexual alternative lifestyles, how to protect yourself from std's, and I just simply am not prepared to answer some of the questions they ask. It is really an area parents ought to be involved in as to when they want to instruct their children and what to say to them. Besides, I've noticed they have been taking liberties with each other in the hallways. I'm pretty sure some of them are already having sex, and no wonder...we teach them how to do it and stir up their passions at a really early age. Ok, I'm through with my rant."

"Nell, get me something to work with. Talk to teachers on the QT. They need to know they won't lose their jobs if they share their mind with you."

"OK, will do then."

Bob grinned a devilish grin knowing Nell could not see him.

Nell got busy immediately interviewing teachers she personally knew from kindergarten through the 12th grade. She even met with the guidance counsellor, Mable Lenard. Mable knew things the kids told her in complete confidence, but couldn't reveal their names, only circumstances. It was a real eye-opening conversation concerning the students. She found out immediately that kids did not have a good home environment. All this time, she naively thought parents were kind, caring, loving and interested in their well being like herself. What she found out was just the opposite. Latch key kids were not a thing of the past. In fact, they were left alone more than she thought and from an early age. Kids were used, abused; mentally, verbally, and physically, they were raped by "funny" relatives and friends, disregarded, discarded, isolated, and forgotten. No wonder test scores were down so low, she thought. These kids don't care when the parents are not involved positively in their lives. And, why should they?

What was the real eye-opening, clarifying moment was when Nell began to research the origin of education in America. She went to the library in hopes she could find some not so apparent information. The librarian suggested she start with a book about John Dewey, the so called author of modern education.

She found that the original school house was a one room building with all grades 1st through 12th. The principal reader was the Bible.

The National Education Association (NEA) was formed in 1857, which later merged with the American Teachers Association in 1966. The actual demise of education in America began in 1918 when the NEA came up with Seven Cardinal Principles which stressed humanist ethical values to replace those of traditional religion. John Dewey, a liberal humanist helped draw up the document know as the Humanist Manifesto in 1933. When Nell began to read the Humanist Manifesto, she found the biggest reason for the demise of education in America. The first tenet was: Religious humanists regard the universe as self-existing and not created. (There is no God and the universe is not created). Evolution, then was the accepted theory of creation from that time. My God, she thought, no wonder people think we come from monkeys. Again she thought, In just a little over 80 years, modern education has changed the way we view ourselves since Adam over 6000 years ago. There is no respect for human life and dignity. Death and dying, abortion, euthanasia, and infanticide, and holocausts are just a way of life.... Then the end.

Nell could see all the things our nation was teaching our kids about life mandated by the federal government, and supported by the National Education Association. It was a conspiracy to destroy the name of God and the way of mankind as we know it. She read more of the Manifesto. It denied the existence of the soul, it rejected traditional religion, it asserts humanism as a religion, it rejected capitalism, touted socialism, believed in the redistribution of wealth, supported the teaching of free sex including homosexuality and other perversions, supported birth control, abortion, and divorce, mind control, group manipulation, and any and everything that was contrary to the word of God and sound doctrine.

It was at this moment of clarity that Nell saw how Satan had taken over the minds of school children in America. What with a "foundation of darkness" they got in grammar school and high school, it was easy for her to see how liberal colleges and professors have destroyed what was left of the minds of God's chosen. She was sick! How could this happen? Who else knew? What could be done?

At this juncture of life, Nell vowed, "The Devil is not gonna' have my kids." Back she went to Bob Stogell. "Bob, do you have any idea what the foundation of the National Education Association is?"
"I'm not sure what you are asking me. What are you talking about?"
"I'm talking about what the founding documents of our educational system are. Have you read them?"

"I've read a lot of things. What in particular are you asking me?"

"Have you read the "Humanist Manifesto I, II, & III? These are founding documents of our educational system and have been for over 80 years. Here, I made you a copy. Take this home and read it. It will open your eyes."

"Exactly what am I looking for?"

"Ok, in them you will see that the Humanist Manifesto is essentially the same as Karl Marx' Communist Manifesto worded in a different way. And the Communist Manifesto has the same…the exact same platform as progressive democrats in America. Aren't you a democrat, Bob? And, it is the same platform that Fidel Castro took over Cuba with, and the same platform that this current president has been instituting since he took office. You know, "Hope and Change". Hope and change from what? From a free America with a rule of law to a socialistic America under bureaucrats. I can't stand it. It is not a little conspiracy, it is a complete and total government takeover of every fiber of America. And it came in with a "Trojan Horse". And the "Trojan Horse" is our school system. And the occupants are our unsuspecting kids. And it is working."

"Whoa, slow down, Nell. There has got to be a good explanation."

"I just explained it to you in a nutshell. It's all there. It's like the aliens have landed and they are inhabiting our people. And, I can't help but tell you, I'm not a little pissed off."

"Nell, give me a chance to read all this. It seems like I looked it over a few years ago, but I didn't see all you are telling me."

"Bob, this is not a game. These people are playing for real. And the chips are our children. And they are playing pot limit."

"Ok, Ok, I'll read it and get back to you tomorrow."

"Fine!"

Nell had the go ahead to pursue this path from Bob a few days ago. She was not sure what he would say after he read the documents, but she was determined to go further. She called Buck, her friend. She had taught Buck's kid back seven years ago, and he stood by her when she had disciplined a child who got in a fight with his son. And she thought she could count on him. "Buck, I've heard you and Pastor Jimmy Hawkins have been making quite a stir around here. Y'all have laid out the gauntlet, and stirred up the devil. How about some more action?"

EDUCATION

"Hmmm, what do you have on your mind, Nell?"

Nell then laid out all her findings about the kids and their diminishing grades in school, her findings about lack of discipline with the kids, and her findings about the NEA and the Humanist Manifesto. "Buck, I think it is a hostile takeover by the devil. The ones in charge are the leaders of every aspect of our society. I wonder if you can find anything out about who is responsible for the degradation of our kids in Cedar Falls?"

"Nell, you certainly have my attention. You know I have never backed up from a fight."

"I know! That's why I am calling you. You are a fighter and a supporter of what's fair and just, truth, and equity, and right judgment."

"Well, I don't know if I am all that."

"Well, I'm going to tell you that you are. And you always have been. You just had a spiritual experience and your gifts have exponentially escalated."

"Tell you what. I'll pray about it and let you know what I come up with. Deal?"

"Deal. Let me know as soon as you know."

Buck had to go to City Hall to get a remodeling permit. He was passing by Mayor Tom's office when he saw the Mayor at his desk. He tapped on the door and said, "Hello, Mayor."

"Hello, Buck. How's it going with you?"

"Good. How do you like the new minister at church?"

"I haven't got to speak with him but once and that briefly. Heard you were leaving us."

"Yep. My wife and I decided to start going to Jimmy Hawkins home fellowship."

"You know, Buck, you are a well respected man here in the community. If you start going to that little charismatic group, folks are going to start looking at you differently. Not trying to tell you what to do, but, it would be smart to stay in a mainline religious organization that's got a track record, what with your status in the community and all…"

"Like the Methodist Church?"

"Exactly, like the Methodist Church."

At that moment, Buck saw a totem behind the Mayor's desk. It didn't have the Gargoyle on top, but it was exactly a replica of the one in Pastor Goodman's office. "Where did you get the totem," he asked?

"Oh, you know, I pick up trophies here and there. It's a topic of conversation. When folks come by, we can talk about the Indian influence on this area. It's a great ice breaker."

"I see. Ok, got to go get my permit if I want to do my repairs from the storm. See ya' later."

"Great, Buck. See ya'."

It was disconcerting to say the least for Buck to see the totem in the Mayor's office. But, there were still a lot of Indians around here and their culture had undeniably marked the area. Totems were not a big deal for they were everywhere. Or, were they?

Buck started to leave city hall, walked down the beautiful marble steps past the huge white columns when he heard a shriek above. It sounded like a mixture of a hawk and a crow. As he looked up, this lifesize creature swooped at him and shrieked again. It made another pass. Buck started running for his pick up. The creature swooped again and brushed his head. His sharp talons were extended like a large peregrine going after his prey. It struck him on the shoulder as he passed by, ripped his shirt, and left claw marks in his pecs and his lats. He ran faster, unlocking his truck with his push button keys as he ran. He jumped in as the creature hit the windshield with a thud. Safely inside, Buck cranked up, and pulled out of the parking lot. He looked on both sides, in front and behind, but he didn't see anything. Whatever that hideous thing was, it was gone. And then he began to think, am I hallucinating? Have I gotten into the dark side and my imagination has gone wild with me? And why now? Buck believed the Mayor to be a nice man, but that totem and others like it were getting to be a sign he could not any longer disregard. He made up his mind at that minute that he was going to check the Mayor out a little further. If there was something going on, he had to know.

Buck started ruminating in his mind all of the things that had happened of recent dates. There was a murder, suicide, fornication, prostitution, adulteries, drunkeness, drug use, the occult, lies, deceptions,

EDUCATION

homosexuality, pedophilia, idolatry, and God only knows what else he thought. How could all these things be in this sleepy town? Why, he was even caught up in some of it. And, how long had all this been going on? Was it possible that this creature was responsible for all the sins and improprieties or was it man who was evil and the devil just spurred it on? All he knew at this time was that it had to end. The devil was not going to get these school kids, too.

Buck called Nell. "How's the project coming, Nell?"

Buck, there has to be a conspiracy involved. I don't know how, but it appears to me it has to come from the top. If it were grass roots, some of the people I have talked to would know something about it. It is just the opposite. They are totally ignorant of any of the things I showed Bob. In fact, they have never heard of any such thing."

"How do you think we need to proceed?"

"Do you think you can go to the courthouse and look up political affiliations in the registrar of voter's office? It might be a start. Begin with Democrats or Progressives, then Socialist or Communists. There has to be clue here somewhere because they are too closely aligned to be a mistake. And they have to know what their party believes in. I'm not talking about the common people. They are just mice led by the Pied Piper. Look for leaders."

"Like leaders....umm like Bob or the Mayor or the councilmen?"

"Yes! Make a list before you go. If they are registered as any of those affiliations, it may be they have ties somewhere else. Then we can look at archives of former socialists or communists on Google maybe. We have to start somewhere. We can probably eliminate at least half of them from the search if they are conservatives, patriots, tea partiers, or republicans, NRA members, or Christians."

"Ok! Will do. Get back with you later."

Buck went to the court house like Nell suggested and went to the registrar of voters office. Since it was all public record, he could look to his heart's content. But, after four hours of searching, he hadn't found any significant information. He called Nell. "Nell, I looked through the voter records, and I found a lot of democrats here in Cedar Falls. In fact, about one half of the voters are democrats. I really couldn't find any other significant affiliations. Tell you what. I'm going home and get on my computer. The company I sell for is an international company, and they may have something I can use. Lexus Nexus out of Houston has several major offices around the world. They specialize in doing bios on corporations and people from birth to death, which include their ancestry, school records, spouses and children, work history, military history, incarcerations and arrests if any, what they buy and sell, and who they are doing business with including fraternal type organizations. They are who we call when we need to hire or see who we are dealing with. It might be I can get some information from them."

"Ok, sounds like a good idea."

Buck called his boss to see if he could do some research on some organizations and people before he got started. His boss told him the company had a retainer with Lexus Nexus, and he could look to his heart's content. They did have a limit every month on how much or how many searches he could make, but for what he wanted, it wouldn't be enough to pay extra.

As soon as he got on the computer, he started searches on the Bilderbergs. This was a private international company comprised of 150 to 180 world leaders. Due to its privacy, Bilderberg is also accused of conspiracies. This outlook has been popular on both extremes of the political spectrum, even if they disagree about the exact nature of the group's intentions. Some on the left accuse the Bilderberg group of conspiring to impose capitalist domination, while some on the right have accused the group of conspiring to impose a world government and planned economy.

Then he looked up the Illuminati. The Illuminati is a secret organization of the most powerful and influential elite in the world. They go back for centuries and maintain the same bloodlines. They set up the council on foreign relations, the Bilderberg group and the Tri-Lateral Commission. Those three groups all meet to plan the fate of the world. They consist of international bankers, top government officials, leaders in the energy cartel and media monopoly owners and have control over the U.N. and UNESCO. Their subdivisions reach into everyones' daily life without most sheeple even being aware of it. They also have ties to the Freemasons, Skull and Bones, and the Knights Templar. Their ultimate goal is for a one world government which they will control, also a one world currency, and they want control and ownership of all

EDUCATION

land, property, resources and people. Also, they manipulate political parties, and the legal and illegal drug trade and federal agencies related to all matters.

He looked into the Rothschilds, but decided that though they were likely the richest people in the world in the 1800's, their power and wealth had diminished enough that a conspiracy could not be proven about them.

He looked into Free Masons, Jews, the Catholic Church, as well as theories centered on Communism or international capitalists, the Skull and Bones, the Ku Klux Klan, the NAACP, and any other movement that either disrupted society or distracted the mainstream of society from seeing what was going on beneath the radar. After a long search to no avail, he came across the Wiccan.

Buck found out that Wicca was a modern day witchcraft religion. It only developed in England in the middle of the 20th Century. But, it had gained wide spread acceptance in various places including the USA. Buck couldn't really draw a clear distinction between magic, Wicca, and Satanic witchcraft, but it looked like witchcraft involved some type of pact with the devil or a demon or an evil spirit of some kind. Generally, their power was used to kill, awake passions, do their bidding, bring calamity on their enemies, or call up the dead while magic was used for illusion, and Wicca was a more earth-based religion. The Salem witch trials in 1692 had caused 19 people to be executed, and mostly they were women who were believed to be demon possessed. Buck had seen Pastor Jimmy cast out devils, and tell other stories of demon possession. He was already a believer. What Buck had seen already in the form of the Gargoyles made him believe witches were probably real, too. But, who would get involved in the occult, he thought? And what do they do?

Buck did more research and found out that witches like black, have brooms, cats, pointed conical hats, magic wands, potions, tatoos, pentagrams, candles, cauldrons, and enjoy all types of sexual perversions. He had previously thought all these things were fairy tales. They usually met at night in a coven of other witches, and performed their obscene acts. He read where wiccans, witches, and Satanists are everywhere such as government, teachers in schools, churches, business men and women, and children. There was no place they could not reach. He stopped. What they did shocked him. Occultists throughout the country performed occult crimes, including drug peddling, child abduction, rape, pornography, and animal and human sacrifice, They sacrificed on the lowest level chickens, dogs, and cats, and advanced to higher levels of babies, small children, young virgin women, and anyone else that was required to give their blood for the cause. In his pause, he began to reflect on Pastor John Goodman. He was involved in witchcraft, homosexuality, and likely murder depending on the results Sheriff Kelly Vargas got back on the forensics. Buck reasoned, if somebody's conscious was so seared that he practiced witchcraft in the church, then there was no sacred places where it was not practiced. Then it occurred to him. The last person who had anything to do with maybe the occult was the Mayor. He had a totem, though it was not like the one Pastor John Goodman had. The Mayor's didn't have a Gargoyle on top. Maybe yes, maybe no....

Buck called Pastor Jimmy. "Jimmy, how would you like to do some sleuthing with me?"
"What you got on your mind, Buck?"
"Well, I've been doing a lot of research on these witches, Wiccans, and Satanists."
"And...?"
"And, it appears that they do not have much that can be found on Google except what they do. I can't really find any organizations that one can join. So, I decided I would follow the only lead I have at this point."
"You have a lead?"
"It's sketchy, and it may not be anything to it, but I feel like I need to search it out. The Mayor had a totem in his office like Pastor Goodman except without the Gargoyle. He said it was an "ice breaker" to start a conversation with folks who come in his office, and a chance to tell about the Indian history here in Cedar Falls. I, also found out witches meet at night. Like maybe around midnight. What I would like to do since I don't know which night they might meet or how often they go out is just observe the Mayor's house for a week or two each night to see if he goes anywhere...maybe like a meeting with a coven...maybe his coven. It may be a long shot, but it won't hurt to try. What ya' say?"

EDUCATION

"Hey, I'm game. We might not get much rest for a while, but who knows, we might hit the jackpot. Let's do it."

"Ok, we can start tonight. It's Wednesday, a church night, then four days later, it will be Sunday night, another church night. Since they are highly religious, it just seems to me they would do a perversion of Holy days. I'm not ruling out other days, but these we want to really be alert, I feel like."

"Ok, what time do you want to get started?"

"Oh, I think if we got to the Mayor's house around 11:30, maybe it would be about the time he would be leaving. The meeting place can't be too far from his home, at least I don't think."

"That's great! Pick me up around 11:15."

Jimmy got in Buck's brand new black Chevy Silverado. It had a big V-8, power steering, leather and power seats, Sirius, wifi, 4 wheel drive, automatic transmission, special 20" chrome wheels, a chrome package, bed liner, chrome plated truck bed bars, a towing package and plenty other extras. Talk about a tricked-out truck. Jimmy noticed the new smell when he got in. And it drove like a Cadillac...so smooth. All Jimmy had was an old six cylinder, 1999 Ford, single cab truck which had a little slack in the steering, and had logged over 300,000 plus miles. He thought, I could get used to this. But, as a full time Charismatic preacher whose church was at home, there was not much income. If it were not for his wife teaching school and taking some house cleaning jobs, they would not even be able to pay the bills much less buy a new truck. But, they were happy and looked with anticipation of more prosperous days ahead. They pulled up close to the Mayor's house around 11:30 about a block away, rolled down the windows, cut off the lights, and cut the engine. Now all they had to do was wait.

They did not have to wait long. At 11:45, the garage door to the house opened. They could see the Mayor backing out in his beige Lincoln Town Car. Buck cranked the engine, waited till the mayor got about 2 blocks down the street and pulled behind to follow. To their surprise, after about 5 minutes of driving, the Mayor pulled up to a 24 hour Quick Stop Convenience Store. It had a glass front so they could see everything he was doing. After he got his supplies, he paid, got back in his car and drove straight home. He parked outside the garage doors, went inside with his package, and came right back out. Obviously, he had to deliver something to his wife. He got back in his car, pulled out into the street once again, and sped off. "Uh, Oh!" Exclaimed Jimmy. "This is it."

The Mayor drove to the outskirts of town, pulled down a side road and drove about 5 miles. He turned into a dirt drive and drove another mile. Buck could see well enough ahead that he stopped at least a quarter mile away. The Mayor got out of his car, and walked up to an old dilapidated barn. Someone was at the entrance, and let him in immediately. There were about 10 other cars out front, so Buck knew they had to be careful. He pulled off on the side of the road onto another dirt road into a grove of trees that hid his truck out of sight. "Jimmy, we will have to be very careful now. If they are doing anything close to what I read about, these guys and or gals could be dangerous." They got out of their truck, and slipped around the barn where they could not be seen by the lone vigil. There were two windows in the back, one on each side of the building. A six foot hedge and some tall weeds had practically covered them up. Buck said, "You go to that one, and I'll go to this one. Don't get directly in the window. Look from the side. They won't be able to see outside very well, but we can see inside great." The windows were dirty, the weeds were unbearable, and they hoped there were no snakes laying around.

Both men peered in. What they saw was incomprehensible. There were about 20 men and women, all dressed in black gowns with pentagrams monogrammed on their chest, they had big gold necklaces hanging down to the middle of their stomach with an upside down cross hanging from it. The leader obviously was the Mayor. He had a red gown, a crown that looked like spiked goats horns, and a 12" long stiletto type knife. There were candles all on the floor around what looked like a surgeon's stainless steel table. The candles looked different. Buck remembered reading about human sacrifices of little babies. They would take the fat from the body and form their own candles. The table had a linen cloth covering it, and a beautiful young girl weighing maybe 100 pounds strapped to the table with her arms above her head, and her legs stretched wide and strapped down. She was totally naked except for some tape on her mouth. Her eyes were wide with fright. On a platform at the front of the table was a huge silver Pentagram on top of a black drape. Behind the table was a 10' totem with a huge Gargoyle at the top. Suddenly, they all began to chant. The cresendo got louder and louder. The Mayor parted his gown, mounted the young girl. The chanting got louder and louder. The Mayor took some kind of instrument, inserted it into the young girl's vagina, and began to pull out his sperm. It looked like a sizeable amount which he put it in a silver chalice. He then passed it around and each of the wiccans began to sip it. The chanting became a roar. In turn, each of the men mounted the young girl and had sex with her. There were about eight women there who then took off their gowns exposing their total nakedness. They began to circle the table, insert their fingers in her vagina, pull out some sperm and smear it on her and on their own breasts. This all went on about 10 minutes. Buck and Jimmy were appalled. Suddenly, the Mayor hovered over the girl, and began to make a speech. "We have come here tonight to make a sacrifice to Satan by initiating this young virgin into our midst. She has proven herself worthy by giving her virginity to each and every one of us. Her firstborn child which will be conceived here will be sacrificed on this very same altar eight days after it is born. The supreme sacrifice she has and will make is well noted by our god, Satan himself. Then the Mayor raised his knife and slowly lowered it to her breast where he made an incision in the shape of a Pentagram. She now belongs to us forever. The incantations began again, this time at the top of their voices. Each one began to pull off their clothes and began to have a wild orgy on the floor. After they were spent, one by one they got up, put their clothes back on, and began to hug one another. Buck and Jimmy had never read about anything like this, never seen anything like this, and never thought anything like this could really exist. "Let's get out of here," Buck, "I think the party is over."

When they got back to the truck, they backed out and started for home. "I don't think anyone even knew we were around," said Buck. "Now, we have to decide what we are going to do about it." Before he could get his words out of his mouth, a huge black creature came crashing down out of the trees. It had to be over 10' tall itself, had an 8' wingspan, and totally blocked the road. "Uh, Oh, Jimmy, we are in for it now."

Jimmy's eyes got big. He opened his mouth and started to scream, and remembered a scripture, "Be not afraid of sudden fear." He shouted to the top of his voice, "JESUS!" The creature lifted and was gone just that quick.

"Wow! Exclaimed Buck. "There is power in that Name."

While Buck and Jimmy were making their way back home, they were almost totally silent. Buck pulls up to Jimmy's driveway, and said, "Jimmy, If this is the kind of thing Pastor Goodman was involved in, we can surely expect a baby to be sacrificed in nine months. Did you recognize any of the people there?"

"Buck, Sad to say, but, I recognized nearly all of them. There was Pastor Sam Trace's wife who I thought was in jail. Sheriff Vargas was there which explains why Julie was there. Unbelievably, Bob Stogell was there. No wonder the school system was messed up. Ole' Ruby Dixon was there, as well as Sister Anne who was Elder Tom's wife, Farley Metzinger and his wife were there. Betty, another Pentecostal wife was there. I wonder if their husbands know about this. I bet not. Two high school boys, one high school girl, 3 college students, three female grammar school teachers, and one male high school math teacher."

"Jimmy, this is just one meeting and one coven. We don't know if there are more involved or if there is another coven somewhere. I think I am beginning to understand why we have these Gargoyles around. You think they are real Gargoyles or just demons manifested as Gargoyles?"

"Probably just demons, but it really doesn't make any difference. They are just as wicked and unclean."

"I'll tell you one thing...Now, I understand why our school system is failing. You saw our Superintendent in there. He jumped up there on that table and was screwing that little girls brains out, excuse the French. Guess I'm not sanctified yet. She had to be a minor. I didn't recognize her from anywhere I frequent, but she didn't look even 17 years old. Everybody in there could be held for statutory rape. Seeing the Sheriff mount her didn't make me feel real good about our law enforcement either. You know those guys act real nice, seem to do their job, everybody likes them, but I can see how they have stonewalled us on some issues. And now I see why. Well, me and that buddy who is over our kids are going to have a "set to go to" meeting conference real soon. I'm real pissed off that he is over our kids. I don't know if he has a clue about the agenda that Nell has found out, but I'm pretty sure he does."

"Buck, you can't jump in there too soon. We need to get everything on him we can before we start to accuse him of anything. And, besides that, we may need to get the State Police or the FBI in here if we want to bust the Sheriff. He is definitely in violation of the law as well as everybody else we saw. Like I said before, this may not be all of them."

Buck got back with Nell to tell her all about the events of the previous night. "Nell, this thing is worse than you or I even first imagined. The utter depravity of the whole coven meeting made me ill. The Sheriff was there, Bob Stodgell was there and a lot of leading citizens of the community and church leaders. There is definitely a conspiracy going on with the kids. Have you gotten back with Bob about the information you gave him yet?"

"I have, Buck. He told me again that he had read it all a while back, so he hasn't been in a hurry to read it again. He did say he would get around to it. It was kinda' like, don't bother anymore. I'll get around to it when I get around to it. I don't think that he has any intention of reading it at all."

"Nell, I want to find out who that young blonde was that everybody assaulted last night. I have no clue where to start."

"What did she look like?

"She was young, maybe in high school, real cute, a blonde, slim, and relatively short, I'd say about 5' or so, and had black finger and toe nails. She had a tat on her hip and right hand, but I couldn't make it out."

"You know, she sounds just like a junior in high school I have seen around the campus. The grammar school and the high school share the same cafeteria. She is very popular with all the boys. And this girl has black nails, dark make-up, and a tat I think is a pentagram on her hand."

"Wow, that sounds just like her. What's her name? Anita...Anita Beckstrom. Her parents are well to-do, and as far as I know, she is a real handful at home."

"Anita Beckstrom? Hmmmm.... There are some Beckstroms that live past me about two miles. Never met them or their daughter. Think I will take a drive out there and meet them."

Buck went and got Pastor Jimmy. "We've got to meet some folks by the name of Beckstrom that live out past me. I need you to go with me. Their daughter may be the one that was getting screwed all night last night."

"I'm in. Let's go."

Buck and Jimmy drove out to the Beckstrom home that minute. As they approached the driveway, they noticed that the property was protected by a white 6' fiberglass privacy fence with a black double gate made of steel. It was one of those that had an electric eye and a voice box to call the house. The house was magnificent. It looked like it had probably 8,000 square feet of living space, with 6 huge white columns in front. It had beautiful dormers out cropping the second floor. The roof had a multitude of gables and hips, dark brown architectural shingles, and the front had a huge 9' steel door painted red. The house had a beautiful beige and white stone which gave it a massive look like one would find on the signature architectural buildings in Washington D.C. It had a white stone trim at every corner. It was truly a beauty. Buck guessed it probably would cost at least two million to build. Buck punched the button on the box at the gate. A voice came on. "What is your business?"

I'm here to see Mr. Beckstrom and his daughter Anita if they are in. My name is Buck Merriman. I am an agent with an international sales company and live about 2 miles back toward town on this road. I have Pastor Jimmy Hawkins with me from a local Charismatic Church in town."

"Again, what is the nature of your business?"

Buck briefly paused and thought, if I am not completely honest, we won't get in. If I am completely honest and Mr. Beckstrom is in the coven, they wouldn't get in. But, if he wasn't, he just might want to find out what is going on. He chose the latter. "We are trying to find out if Anita was at a coven meeting last night or if it was someone else. I think Mr. Beckstrom would be particularly interested in knowing about her extracurricular activities."

"Hold a moment."

A couple of minutes later the gates opened and Buck and Jimmy drove up to the front door. A man came out in a very nice servant's outfit. He held the door while another man came out in a gray business

EDUCATION

suit, black alligator wing tips, and a red silk tie. Impressive to say the least. "Come in", the gentleman said.

Buck and Jimmy got out of the truck, walked up the stone steps to the porch which had dark brown pavers. The man reached out his hand to shake, and said, "My name is Stephen Beckstrom. Welcome!"

After they all shook hands and said a few formalities, Mr. Beckstrom said, "What can I help you gentlemen with today?"

"Well, sir, it may not be so much what you can help us with, but maybe we can help you."

Beckstrom stepped back in surprise.

Jimmy was the first to speak, "Sir, we were engaged on spying out a meeting last night that may involve your daughter. Since we are not sure, we are slow to speak. Is her name Anita?"

"It is."

"Before we go on, is it possible to see her or a picture of her to confirm what we saw last night?"

"Anita is not here right now, but I do have a picture." He reached in his back pocket, pulled out a billfold, opened it and showed them a picture he had recently taken of Anita. "Is this her, " he asked?

Buck and Jimmy both looked at the picture, looked at each other, then looked at Mr. Beckstrom who by now was totally bewildered. "Has she done something wrong, he asked?

"Mr. Beckstrom, we may need to go in so you can sit down." He led them down a wide hall to a double hidden door which he opened automatically. It was a huge room with shelves on three sides to the ceiling filled with all kinds of books. There was a fireplace on one end of the room with crossed swords above and a family coat of arms. A massive executive desk with four big leather chairs in front and an executive leather chair in back which was Mr. Beckstroms. "Please be seated," he said. "Now what is it that your have to tell me?"

"Mr. Beckstrom…"

"Please call me Stephen."

"Yes, sir! Stephen, we both saw your daughter in a coven meeting, more particularly a Satanist meeting last night. We went there on a hunch that something was not right with a town leader to see if it was anything we needed to be involved in. We sneaked up to the back and looked in the windows. We got much more than we bargained for. A Satanist meeting was going on with about 20 people, your daughter being one of them. She was strapped to a table surrounded by candles and all these other people, both men and women. Mr. Beckstrom, this is the hard part. She was naked on that table, and each one of the men in that room had her. The leader said something along the lines that if she conceived that they would sacrifice the baby eight days after it was born. From what we saw, we believe it all to be true."

Beckstrom was speechless. His face turned red, and tears began to come to his eyes. He tried to talk, but all he could do was stutter and bawl. Finally, after he began to regain his composure, he said, "Are you sure?"

"Sir, we are sure from the picture you showed us that the girl that was being abused was your daughter."

"My God! What can I do? My daughter has a stubborn streak. We have tried to talk to her, take her to church, teach her the right things, but I'm afraid we have indulged her too much."

"Mr. Beckstrom, we need your help."

"Anything! Support, help, service, man power, money...Anything! I want my daughter back."

"Sir, we believe this coven has its claws in a multitude of local people, business men, clergy, and officials, and that many children have been enlisted into this organization including your daughter. We think she didn't really know what she was getting into, for she had fear in her eyes. She was strapped down and had no choice. What we want to do is stop this insanity in our town, and keep these kids from getting involved in the occult and being raped."

"What do you want me to do?"

"If you have any connections with the State Police or the FBI...."

"I do!"

"Then, let's call them up. This may not only be city wide or county wide, but this may actually cross state lines. I think we have been infiltrated from the top down."

That evening, Mr. Beckstrom's daughter came home from spending time with her friends. She went straight to her bedroom. Beckstrom tapped on her door and entered without asking if he could come in. Anita was sitting on her bed with her legs crossed. She looked up at her Dad slowly only to see big tears in his eyes. "You know don't you?" She said.

EDUCATION

"I do. Can I help you with anything?"

"Oh, Daddy," as she began to sob. "I am so sick of what I have done. I had no idea what I really was getting into. I thought everything was so cool to be called a witch. I certainly didn't know the price I would have to pay. I have been so violated, and I may have allowed stuff to happen to me that I can't reverse. I'm afraid my life is ruined."

"Not so, honey. Daddy is going to help you work all this out. We will need to take some positive action though, if you think you can help me."

"I will do anything you say. I just want this nightmare over."

Beckstrom went over the plans with his daughter right then. "First, we are going to get you examined to see if you are pregnant. Then we are going to file rape charges against your violators. I'm calling the FBI. There is a long time friend in there I went to school with. He can do the investigation. We will get you some private counseling for I am sure you have some major issues to deal with. It will be good. It doesn't mean you are crazy or anything like that, but you may need to be reprogrammed somewhat. We will need your testimony as to the things that happened that night as well as other nights if any, how you got recruited, what you had to learn to become a coven member, and to testify in court against those perps. Are you up to all that?"

"I am. Let's do it."

Beckstrom didn't become rich because he was ignorant. In fact, he was a brilliant man, and knew important people all over the world. He realized early on that it paid to get special favor in a time of crisis. He called Alec Haskell, his good school buddy who was now high up in the FBI. "Alec, I have a problem." After talking for over 30 minutes, Alec had gotten as much scoop as he needed.

"Stephen, I'm going to clear my calendar as best I can, book a flight, and I should be there in three days. Is that good with you?

"It certainly is, Alec. I'm so glad you are going to take a personal interest in this. I really appreciate it."

"Well, I will tell you what, I think y'all may have uncovered a big operation. And this kind of stuff is right up my alley. See you in three days."

Beckstrom got in touch with Buck and Jimmy and told them about talking with his friend in the FBI. He also told them about his conversation with his daughter, Anita, and how willing she was to help. Buck called Nell to inform her how fast things were moving now. "Nell, I think we may actually get something done here. Don't say anything else to Bob Stogell, though. He is in on all this and so is Sheriff Vargas. And God only knows who else."

Stephen Beckstrom got in touch with Buck and Jimmy, and had them contact Nell. He told them to bring pen and paper because it was going to be an exploration session. Anything they could come up with would be given to the FBI. He informed his wife Jenny about everything that was going on. She, of course, was devastated. "Where did we go wrong? Oh, God, please tell me what I have done wrong."

Before she could get into a pity party, Stephen stopped her. "Honey, nobody has been a bad parent. Anita just was testing the reins some, the same thing you and I did when we were young. What happened was bad, but we can all get through this. Just remember, it all happened to Anita, not to you and not to me. It's about her and not us. Got it."

"I got it. You always know how to settle me down."

The day before Alec was to arrive, they all met at the Beckstrom's house including Anita. As they went through the huge double doors, all they could do was oooh and ahhh. The inside was extravagant to say the least. Every wall was 12 feet tall except for the living area. It was 30 feet tall overlooked by the second floor with an exquisite four foot wrought iron rail hand made by local artisans. Every ceiling was recessed with huge chandeliers hanging half way to the floor. The moulding was twelve inches wide and not a joint from one end to another. Every wall had very beautiful and valuable renaissance paintings, and decorated with huge gold mirrors and artifacts from around the world. The floors were stone and wood, and all the cabinets were a beautiful beige marble. All stainless steel appliances were found in the kitchen. As they entered the den which measured twenty feet by twenty feet, it had the feeling of authority. It had a huge cherry stained 4x6 executive desk, a log fireplace at one end surrounded by plush couches and leather reclining chairs.

"Have a seat, please," he said. Everybody gathered around and began to talk suddenly at once.

EDUCATION

Pastor Jimmy, with a loud voice over the din, said, "I think we need to pray. This is a very important meeting and we need God's grace to be with us." To which everyone solemnly nodded.

After prayer, Beckstrom began to lay out the plan and quickly engaged everyone to write down every thing they could think of. They were all informed of his conversation with Alec Haskell, the FBI agent. Alec, he told them would be in town tomorrow, and would need all the information they could give him. Also, he told them that he would likely question each and everyone to get a better feel for everything. It sounded to Buck like he had been through something like this before. And, of course, he had, only on a bigger scale, international espionage.

The next day, Alec had flown into the airport, got his bags and a rental car, and headed to the Beckstroms. Everybody was there waiting on him. The first thing he said after he got them all assembled was, "Anita, you are going to be the star witness in all this. Are you, or do you think you are up to all this?"

"Yes, Sir."

"Very good then. Give me just a moment to retrieve my tape recorder. Now, tell me all you know. Anita handed him the information she had put on paper from the day before. Then she began to speak. What she said stunned them all. She had been in this cult for a year, but never engaged in a ritual. There were prominent citizens from Cedar Falls and surrounding towns that were all associated with this particular coven. She gave names, dates, events, training, and had a list of books she personally had in the trunk of her car. She always had to be careful not to let her parents see them. She also told him about other kids and their names that had been recruited all the way down to grammar school. After her testimony, Alec cut off his recorder. Ladies and gentlemen, we have enough information from Anita here to bust this whole thing. If all her facts line up with other potential testimonies, I believe we can hand your town back to you.

"Praise God!" Jimmy exclaimed.

"Praise God!" said Buck.

"Praise God!" said them all.

Alec, immediately getting back to his room called his Washington headquarters. The J. Edgar Hoover Building is a high-rise office building located at 935 Pennsylvania Avenue NW in Washington, D.C containing over 64 acres of office space. It was built in the Nixon era, and resembled a fortress without windows. It could certainly not be pillaged. But, over the years, it had lost its architectural aesthetic. It did not blend in with the surrounding buildings and according to some, it had lost its usefulness. It was time to get new office space somewhere else. Plans were in the process. Alec didn't think he would be around long enough to enjoy the new facilities, but who cares? He loved his job and he was good at it. "Get me about ten agents out here ASAP," he said. "We have a big case and a lot of people are going down, and I need the help."

Alec's superior immediately dispatched 10 agents to Cedar Falls. As soon as they arrived, Alec led a task force of two to Bob Stogell's office. Alec was in a suit, but his two agents were dressed in SWAT clothes. They made a scary appearance and invoked fear on all who looked upon them. They entered the School Board office at 10:00 AM. The secretary said, "May I help you?"

Alec said, "Is Mister Stogell in?"

"He is. Whom may I say is calling?

"My name is Alec Haskell. I am with the FBI."

"One moment, please. I will let him know you are here."

The secretary paged the Superintendent. Alec could hear over the speaker when he said, "Give me a moment."

They had been waiting about five minutes when Alec looked at the Secretary and asked if she knew what the delay was. She did not. "Page him again," he said. Alec did not like to be kept waiting, especially if he thought he was being stonewalled.

"Mr. Stogell....Mr. Stogell....Mr. Stogell...He doesn't seem to be answering."

"Is there a door to the outside from his office?"

"Why, yes it is."

"Let's go, guys. We got a runner." They hurried into the Superintendent's office to find it vacant and the outside door wide open. He had left his suit coat on the rack and some keys on the desk. He had certainly left in haste. Ok, he left some keys. I think one of them is a key to an automobile. He may be totally on foot. Let's catch him." They all hustled outside, and looked right and left. They saw someone running in the distance straight in front of them. It had to be

Stogell. "One of you go get the car. We will pursue and keep an eye on him. Swing around the back here and pick us up as quickly as you can." It was just minutes and the agent had pulled his vehicle around the back and only had to drive about 4 blocks to catch up. Alec still had Stogell in sight. "There he is. Let's get him now." They barreled down on Stogell, pulled up behind him, and spoke over the car bullhorn. "Stop, Mr. Stogell." Stogell quit running and stood with his shoulders slumped and his head down. Alec got out of the vehicle, approached slowly, and said, "You are under arrest, Mr. Stogell for the rape of a minor, Unlawful Flight to Avoid Prosecution, Un-American Activities, and conspiracy to defraud and undermine the government. He read him his Miranda rights, then asked him if he knew and understood what he just said. Stogell nodded yes. "Cuff him, guys."

By now, a group of school employees had gathered outside. Joe was walking by the school grounds when the FBI car came by. His eyes caught Stogell's. Suddenly, Stogell began to sob profoundly. The school employees saw Stogell in the backseat of the FBI car as they drove away. His head was down and he would not make eye contact with any of them. He was totally shamed.

The next day, Blane Fisk, Assistant Superintendent of the School Board called an emergency meeting. There were six members of the board in attendance with one apparent absentee. The board room was plain with yellow tile floors, white walls, no ceiling or floor trim, and no decorations. There were 5-8' tables in the form of a "C". Blane sat at the head of the table. Behind him was the American Flag and the State Flag. He had a small portable table podium with a microphone attached, and quickly called the meeting to order. He asked Johnny Sechler to open in prayer. Everyone rose and bowed their heads. Tom's prayer was very sincere. He asked for God to guide their actions and their minds to make important decisions affecting all the children in Cedar Falls. He ended with a very demonstrative "Amen" to which all chimed in "Amen".

Blane explained to the board the previous day's events in which Bob Stogell had been arrested by the FBI. He even gave an account of Bob's extra curricular activities including his involvement with a coven of witches and the rape of a young woman whose name he withheld. "Ladies and gentlemen," he began, "We are currently without a leader on the school board. I know that as the Assistant Supervisor, I currently have that position. However, I will not be able to fulfill the Superintendent's position on a permanent basis due to my business which takes me overseas from time to time. Nevertheless, it behooves us to select and appoint someone to fill that slot until the next election two years from now in November. I have prayed about this through the night all the way up to this meeting. I believe I have a candidate that I think you could all support. It is a woman who is a fifth grade teacher in our system by the name of Nell Risinger. Nell has a Master's Degree in Education, with a minor in Business Administration. She is very diligent in all she does, she loves kids first and foremost, and it was by her investigation into the present matter that we have been able to go to the source of our educational problems and put an end to them. I believe with all within me that she is to be our next Supervisor of Education. I open the floor for discussion."

Almost at once, they all were in agreement. "Awesome choice," one said, "A brilliant woman", said another, "Good pick", exclaimed another.

"Very well, then, let's take it to a vote. All in favor signify by saying "AYE", and raising your right hand." In unison, they all said AYE and raised their right hands. Blane then said, "Now we have to contact her and see if she will take the position. If she declines, we will meet again and pick someone else. Johnny, perhaps you could go with me to ask her. And if y'all don't mind, I'm going to ask Buck Merriman to go with us. He and Nell have been working on all this from the get go as I appreciate it, and I'm sure he will heartily agree to our choice, and be there to help compel Nell in making this choice." They all agreed and the meeting was adjourned.

That very evening, Blane, Johnny, and Buck went to Nell's house. It was about 5:30 when they knocked on the door. Nell opened up dressed in straight line, light blue cotton dress with a small "V" neck, and sleeves half way to the elbow. She looked much like an angel. "Gentlemen, to what do I owe the privilege of having you at my home? Please come in. Nell seated them in her living room, one on her fold out recliner, and the other two on her couch. She sat straight up with the best of posture on the edge of a straight back chair with her legs crossed.

Blane began to speak. "Nell, you know all about the plight that the School Board has been in the last several days, and by now you know of the Bob's arrest by the FBI. What you don't know is that the Board had a meeting this morning discussing the appointment of our next Supervisor. It was unanimous by one and all that you should take that position. What say you?"

Nell was flabbergasted. She could not talk and began to sputter. "I am overwhelmed," she said. "Why did you choose me?"

Blane went on, "Nell, I prayed all night concerning this, and I believe you are the Lord's choice. And all the members of the board believe that as well. You are well educated, love kids, have their best interest at heart all the time, and are dedicated to their education now and in the future. We all believe you are the best qualified in every point."

Silence ensued for a moment. All eyes were on Nell waiting for her answer. "Gentlemen, I am honored to be selected as the Superintendent of Cedar Falls. I know I can fulfill that job very well and take all the kids in the Cedar Falls district to the next level of education. In fact, I have a lot of ideas on how that is to be accomplished. I accept."

They all began to applaud. Nell turned red in the face embarrassed by the acclamation she had just received. "We will tell the Board first thing in the morning. We will get a substitute immediately for your fifth grade class. Be ready to report to the main office in the morning to take over your duties as the new Superintendent. We will not waste any time," Blane remarked with a big grin on his face.

Buck said, "Nell, knowing you all these years, and watching you in action makes me acutely aware that you are definitely God's best choice. I believe we will see education go to new heights in Cedar Falls. Congratulations!"

4
GOVERNMENT

Mayor Tom Berkley was sitting in his office when he heard Bob Stogell had been arrested. He pushed the button on his office pager to speak to his secretary, Dency. "Dency, clear my calendar for the next five days. I need to take a little time off to plan for the new industrial park the council is proposing."

"Yes, sir! Anything else you want me to do?"

"Just let anyone that calls know that I will be out of town for a few days. I'll should be back by Saturday week."

"Will do."

Tom had a cabin in the mountains that he thought he might go to. The only person he took up there was his wife and occasionally one of his girlfriends. Besides them, no one else knew of his little paradise escape from reality. He called his wife, Betsy. "Bet, pack me a suitcase for a week. I'm going to the cabin. And, I need to be alone to think about this industrial park if you don't mind."

"Oh, no, that is all fine. I can't go anyway. I have meetings scheduled all week, and can't change them out. You go and have a good restful week or so. Hope you get a lot done."

Fifteen minutes later, Tom is driving up to his house. Betsy already had his bags packed. She brought them out to him as he drove up. "You trying to get rid of me," he asked.

"No, I just heard the tone of your voice and knew you needed to get away. Here's all your clothes. Also, I packed you some snacks and drinks along with wine and Old Charter. You won't lack for the niceties of life while you are off thinking.... Except for me that is. But, I will be here when you get back."

Tom kissed her on the cheek and said good bye and gave her a big hug. All the while, he was thinking, I won't miss you either. I have some some stuff you know not of. Besides Tom and Betsy had not had sex in several months. She had some kind of bleeding condition, and would need her ovaries taken out. The earliest doctor's appointment for the operation was still one month away. Tom was not going to let his wife's physical condition keep him from intimacy.

On the way to the cabin, Tom grabbed his cell phone and dialed Sister Anne of the Pentecostal Church. "Anne, I am going up to the cabin for a week or so. You interested in meeting me there?"

"When are you leaving?"

"I am on the way as we speak."

"My husband is going to Las Vegas on a business trip beginning tomorrow for a week. I will see you tomorrow night."

"Sounds good. See you then."

On the way to the cabin, Tom had plenty of time to think about Bob Stogell, the coven meetings, and his involvement in raping a minor. In his mind, he thought he had been given a pass. They got Bob he thought. And, if they really wanted me, they would have been at my doorstep the same hour. Surely, no one knew about the coven. It was a great secret. Bob must have been arrested for some impropriety in office. But, what could that be, he opined? Maybe, it was some kind of malfeasance in office or embezzling school board funds or both. He knew for sure he was stealing money right from underneath the board's nose. In fact, he himself was getting his fair share of the federal grant money coming in for new construction of school buildings. It all had to pass from the Mayor's office before it went to the School Board. He knew he couldn't take the federal check and cash it, so he would deposit them and write a check to his office, then take out his part personally as administrative maintenance. It was the perfect set up. He used three different banks and no one was the wiser. Feeling real good about himself, he began to sing an old Johnny Cash song, "I Hear the Train A Comin' " also known as "Folsom Prison". Little did he think this might define his future.

In the meantime, Alec Haskell met with Stephen Beckstrom, Buck Merriman, Jimmy Hawkins, and Anita Beckstrom in Stephen's home again. Alec said, "Look guys, this investigation is uncovering a lot of things even beyond here that I cannot even tell you about. It's bigger than you can possibly imagine. We do have a case against the Mayor, but he has skipped town. His secretary says he will be gone a little over a week. By now, he probably thinks he is free, but he will be listening to the news wherever he is and may ultimately realize he is hunted as well. The case against a powerful elected official is tougher than against the School Board Superintendent or anybody else for that matter. For this reason, we have to be more circumspect. Anita, I'm not trying to embarrass you or make you feel bad, but one more time, did you know it was the Mayor that raped you first?"

"Yes, sir! No question about it."

"And Buck, you and Jimmy followed him from his house to the barn where the coven meeting was?"

"Yes, sir!"

"And you saw him take his clothes off and rape Anita?"

"Yes, sir!"

"Ok, so y'all will know, we have enough to get this bastard for rape of a minor. Problem is, he may only get a little over 11 years and get out in 5 for good behavior. And he may get off altogether if the act was consensual which it wasn't. But, you never know what a jury will think. I want to nail this son of a bitch for a long time. Do any of y'all know anything else that the good Mayor has done in office that would need investigation."

Buck spoke up. "Well, it has been rumored that he launders money ear marked for city and school projects. Not sure how he does it or even if he does, but I have some good sources. All that said, we could say that about a lot of public officials."

Alec interrupted, "Ok, give me all the information and leads and names you have that could or would divulge information about him.

We will get started immediately. Oh, and he can run for a while, but he can't hide. We will find him."

The next day, Tom was resting on his couch in only a terry cloth robe at the cabin when a knock came on the door. He got up, went to the window and looked out between the blinds. It was Anne. He went to the door and opened it. She came in and gave him a great big hug. "Good to see you, big boy," she said. "Hope you can handle me."
"Oh, I have plans for you, sweetheart. Don't you worry about that. Come on in."
"I have missed you," she said.
"And I have missed you," he answered.
"I couldn't wait to get here. I am so ready, I'm about to explode."
The fire in the fireplace was roaring. A white bear skin rug was laid out right in front of the fireplace. The mantle was a rough hewn, unpainted 6"x 12" oak. The walls were made of rustic enameled logs, and it had a vaulted wood ceiling with 4"x6" beams. It was a cabin in the truest sense, but it had central heat and air, and all the modern kitchen conveniences. It had the appearance of quaint nostalgia.
Tom knelt down on the rug, bent over her so very slowly. In his mind, he thought, Why can't my wife be this hot? But, she had never been. The only thing she did was make love as an act of obedience, never out of passion. This was different, he thought. This woman was born to please a man. This was what heaven was supposed to be like. There was not a care in the world.

Alec Haskell had one of the best FBI field teams in the nation. There were agents exceedingly adept in their own abilities, and they excelled. He had accountants, computer whiz's, forensic experts, scientists, weapons, bomb, and demolition experts, not to mention his SWAT team who was not afraid of anything. He went to a federal judge to get a subpoena for the city's accounting records, and any records that the Mayor kept at his office whether they were public or personal. Alec's main focus was to see if the Mayor was laundering or embezzling money from the city or the federal government. It didn't take long for his team of experts to figure out that he was definitely pigeon holing money into his personal account. The Mayor thought he was pretty smart getting away with all that money he stole, but these guys were experts trained to know and spot inconsistencies in good accounting practices. Within four hours, they had already found where the Mayor had stolen five hundred thousand dollars. The city and the school board were getting millions in federal grants, and the Mayor thought nobody would be the wiser. He paid the city auditors handsomely to turn their heads when they would do the annual audits.

"Ok, boss, we have enough information now that we can get this SOB with a 10 to 30 year sentence plus a hefty fine over $250,000. There is no doubt he stole the money. His fingerprints are on every transaction," Buddy Palmer, the accountant stated.

"Good," Alec said, "Just keep looking. I want everything you can find on this guy."

"Yes, Sir!"

"Barry, have you found anything on his involvement with this coven Buck and Jimmy exposed?"

"Yes, Sir," Barry chimed. We've interrogated Bob Stogell thoroughly. He is trying to plea bargain with us now. He is really a whimp, doesn't want to go to prison, and is willing to confess all for immunity. We've got a pretty good list of people involved, locations of meetings, and their agenda already. It appears this thing spans over 10 cities and towns in different states. We're not sure how much further. We can get him for "Over Throw of the Government" about 20 years, and "UnAmerican Activities" for about 5 years. Along with rape, embezzlement, malfeasance in office, and theft of public funds, he should get a lot of jail time."

"Good work, guys! Now, let's go after the sheriff."

Alec loved bustin' corrupt officials. He couldn't stand a liar, a thief, or a child abuser especially one that was a cop. It appeared each one of the so called respected officials in Cedar Falls was everything he despised. With the news that the investigation might spill over into other cities, towns, and states, he was getting pumped. He especially loved to embarrass them. "I got an idea," he said. Why don't we pay Mrs. Berkeley a visit? Chances are, she doesn't have a clue what all her husband is into, and she may need waking up."

Alec got two of his swat team to follow him, picked up Buck, and drove to the Berkeley's residence. He and Buck walked up to the front door and rang the doorbell. Mrs. Berkeley opened the door and was

GOVERNMENT

surprised to see Buck and a law enforcement officer standing there. Her eyes got big. "Can I help you gentlemen?"

"You sure can, Mrs. Berkeley. May we come in?"

"Of Course!" She opened the door wide, ushered them in, and asked, "Can I get y'all some coffee or coke or tea?"

"No, Ma'am, we are here on business and this might not take long. Mrs. Berkeley, let me get straight to the point. Your husband has been involved in some serious issues that we are investigating involving his tenure in office. May I speak candidly?"

"Sure, what kind of issues? My husband has always been upstanding in everything he has ever done."

"Yes, Ma'am, I'm sure that is exactly what he wants you to see."

"Well, please tell me. What do you say he is involved in."

"Mrs. Berkeley...."

"Please call me Betsy."

"Ok, Betsy, it appears he has been embezzling and stealing funds from the government, participating in un-American activities, involved in a coven and rape of a juvenile for starters."

"Oh, my goodness, that is not possible. I know my husband. He would never do any of that."

"That is why I brought Buck Merriman here, Mrs. Berkeley, uh, Betsy. Buck watched him rape a young girl, and we have agents outside that have gone over the city's books proving beyond a doubt that he is embezzling funds."

"I am sick. I don't believe it, but I hear you talking. How can this be? And what can I do?"

"Betsy, do you have any idea where he is? He has dropped off the radar for us, but we thought you might know."

"Oh, yes, he went up to the cabin... he said to think about the new Industrial Park coming into Cedar Falls."

"The cabin? Can you tell us how to get there?"

"Well, no, I'm not good with telling directions. But, I can lead you there. Will that help?"

"Yes, Ma'am. When can you be ready. Time is of essence."

"I can leave now. Let me get my overcoat."

Tom and Anne had moved to the bedroom and made love several more times.

In the meantime, Alec, Buck, Betsy, and the two SWAT team members pulled up about 50' from the cabin somewhat out of sight. "Look, I don't know what to expect, so let's ease up keeping low till we can better assess the situation."

"I have a key," Betsy said.

"Good, then we don't need a search warrant."

They slipped up to the front door while the two SWAT team members went around the back. Betsy put the key in, slowly opened the door, and walked in. They no sooner got in when they began to hear moans coming out of the bedroom. Betsy headed straight there. She crashed through the door to find Anne and Tom in a wild embrace. "Get out of here, you whore," She screamed. "You get up, you SOB," she hollered as she headed for him.

"Whoa," Alec said. We can take it from here. Buck, go get those agents to come inside. We need to put some cuffs on this mother."

Betsy was fit to be tied. She was screaming and cussing something Tom had never heard in their 25 years of marriage. "I'm going to cut you," she screamed again. "I can't believe you were making love to this Jezebel. Please don't try to tell me this is the first time, either."

The two agents came in and Alec began to speak. "Mayor Tom Berkeley, I am arresting you for the crimes of rape, malfeasance in office, theft, embezzlement, un-American activities, and conspiracy to overthrow the government. He then read him his Miranda rights. Do you understand what I have just told you?" The Mayor hung his head and shook yes. "I need to hear you say, 'Yes', Mayor that you have understood."

"Yes, I understand."

They got him to put some clothes on, turned him around, put the cuffs on him and was about to take him out to the car when Betsy charged. "You, SOB, why have you done this? She began to flail him with her fists. Alec was a little slow in containing her. He felt she may need to vent some.

Slowly, Alec walked around to pull Betsy away. "Take it easy, little lady. The law has him now." She hit him one more time in the face with all she had. It bloodied his nose and mouth.

"I deserved that," the Mayor said. "I'm sorry, Betsy, but you never had sex with me like this."

"What, you are comparing me to this slut? How dare you," and she started at him again. Buck pulled her back.

"It's ok now, Mrs. Berkeley. He is not going anywhere." With that, she was quite and sobbing.

"What are you going to do with Sister Anne here, Alec?" Buck asked.

"Well, she hasn't broken any laws here except commit adultery. Nothing on the books for that. Unless she is involved in something else?"

"She was at that coven meeting that night Jimmy and I saw them."

"Ok, put the cuffs on her, too. We will sort it all out when we get back to town. Read her rights to her, Barry."

"Yes, Sir."

On the way back to town, something fell out of a tree and hit the back of the FBI car. Blammm, it went. Before Alec could speak, something else hit the front of his vehicle. Blammm, it dented his hood. "What th....?" Alec was about to say when they were hit twice more.

Buck remembered what Jimmy had done, and he hollered out, "Jesus," and quickly as the assault had begun, it ended.

"What the devil was all that, t-h-h-h-osse grotesque things?" Alec asked.

"Those, my friend, Alec, is the reason we have so much evil around here. Best I can tell you is that they are demons manifested as Gargoyles. And they are certainly wicked."

"This certainly puts a new twist on our investigation," Alec said. "But, I've got tell you, there is not a judge in the continental USA who will hear a case based on demon oppression or possession. They need concrete facts, not spiritual information. Otherwise, everybody would say, the devil made me do it. Hahaha!"

Things had been really busy for a while, it was Saturday, and Buck was needing some rest. He asked Susie to fix a picnic lunch and go to the lake with him, which she hastily complied. Buck had purchased a hundred acre piece of paradise several years ago, and he and Susie and family went there as often as time would permit. As they drove up, he could see the ten acre lake that had been dug out 20 years ago and was fed by 2 underground cold springs. Buck had hauled in 50 yards of sand to make a private beach for aesthetics and relaxation. It was like being on the ocean and on an inland lake at the same time. He had built a covered dock and pier and put a diving board on the end for swimming. The lake was teeming with wildlife such as ducks flying in from the south, squirrels running from the trees to the water's edge to get a drink, and lots of rabbits. It was full of fish, and on this day, they must have been feeding for the water rippled continuously as bass and bream smacked the water catching the hatch of mayflies, and worms falling out of many trees with webs of larvae. The water was relatively calm, and it was a perfect day. Buck had made a picnic table that would hold 10 people. And, of course, whatever he built was on a grand scale. Susie pulled out a blue plastic sheet and covered the table. She began to cover it with sandwich meat, bread, tomatoes, lettuce, mayonnaise, and mustard. She got the ice chest out full of an assorted mixture of cold drinks including some beer for Buck which he only drank on occasions like this. She pulled out the lawn chairs as Buck was coming from a walk back from the pier. Life was grand and so relaxing. But, it was not destined to stay that way.

A big black truck and a dark blue Cadillac full of people came roaring down the dirt road leading to the lake. They pulled up within 20' of the picnic table with dirt and dust rolling all over their nicely spread table. Alec Haskell got out of the truck, while Jerry Sapp, John Bass, and Dooley Mears, all City Councilmen got out of the Cadillac. "Morning, Buck, morning, Susie", they all said.
"Good morning, fellas," Buck exclaimed. "To what do I have the honor of this visit this fine day?"
Jerry said, "Well, Buck, we have come here to give you a proposition."
"Hmmmm, what kind of proposition?"
"Buck, you know the Mayor went down and it looks like he won't be getting out of jail for a long time pending the outcome of his trial that is. The town of Cedar Falls is currently without leadership, but we can't stop doing business just because the Mayor is in jail. We must go on. Soooo....!'
"Soooo?" replied Buck.
"Sooo, John and Dooley and I were discussing what to do next. Your name came up in the conversation. We talked about what a successful business man you are, your moral and godly characteristics, and what a good family man you are, and what a great leader you are amongst the citizenry here in Cedar Falls. We need to fill Tom's unexpired term.

GOVERNMENT

And we don't need an election. We can appoint an interim replacement just with our vote. Our question is, would you be interested in filling the unexpired term of Tom?"

There was silence for about a minute as Buck and Susie digested what they just heard. Then Buck cleared his throat, and said, "Gentlemen, I am honored that y'all have considered me for this position. You know I am out of the country sometimes for a couple of weeks at a time. I could never fill a position like that on a full time basis which is what you think you may need. Besides, I make much more money than what the Mayor's position pays, and simply could not step over a dollar to make a dime. No disrespect intended."

"Ok, we have considered all that. How about taking the position on a part time basis?"

"Hmmmm, now that is interesting. I'll tell you what, I would do that if you don't require me to have set office hours, if I can go in and out at will, and if you will allow me to pick my staff."

"Sure, we thought you might say something like that."

"Ok, then, one other thing. I already make good money and I won't need a paycheck. If you don't mind, I would like for you to allow me to use the money you would pay me so I could hire a couple of good administrators I trust."

"Sure! No problem. I don't think we even need to meet on that."

Alec Haskell was saving the hardest to last. He needed to bust Sheriff Kelly Vargas and nail his rear end to the wall. One thing Alec did not like was a corrupt cop. He knew he could get him indicted on statutory rape of a minor, aiding and abetting a potential felon, corruption in office, and maybe a couple more charges. But, his main goal was to get him for murder, child pedophilia and homosexual acts with a minor, and possibly child pornography. He only needed to get the fingerprints on that knife that belonged to Pastor John Goodman, see if the knife fit the knife wounds of the skulls of the small bodies that was found behind the Methodist Church, and which was a big and, get the evidence that Sheriff Vargas obtained when the site was scoured for clues before he arrived in town. He figured Vargas would stone wall him or destroy the evidence as quickly as possible especially if it would incriminate him. Considering that Vargas would be a hostile witness or participant in the crime, he didn't think he would hand the evidence over willingly if at all. So, Alec put in a call to the local federal judge to get a subpoena to search the sheriff's office and his home. The subpoena was faxed to his portable fax machine in his truck within the hour. It was getting late in the afternoon, so he gathered up two of his best SWAT team and headed to the Sheriff's office. They were closed. Then it was off to his house. Kelly lived in a three bedroom log home on two acres of land just outside of the city limits. It had a mailbox shaped like a cowboy boot laying on its side. The yard was sparsely landscaped with some hedges on each side of the front door. There were no flowers. The yard was in need of mowing and looked pretty rough in places especially where Bahia grass was growing which was mostly everywhere. He had an attached one car carport where his truck was parked. When Alec drove up, he saw smoke coming from the rear of the house. He had his agents cover each side of the house, and he walked up slowly to the front door. After he rang the door bell, he could hear shuffling inside and momentarily the door opened. A woman in a wheel chair met him at the door.

"Good evening, may I help you?" She said.
"Yes, Ma'am, my name is Alec Haskell and I am with the FBI."
"What can I do for you, Agent Haskell?"
"I'm looking for Sheriff Vargas. Is he home?"
"Of course. I'm his wife and he is out back grilling some hamburgers. Come on in. You can go through the double sliding doors to the back of the house to see him. Can I get you something to drink?"
"No, Ma'am, I'm good. I just need to talk to your husband for a minute."

Mrs. Vargas had a car wreck ten years ago and it had left her partially paralyzed. A drunk driver had crossed the center line and hit her head on. She was very fortunate to be alive. This accident was the main reason her husband had run for office in the first place to put criminals, felons, and drunks behind bars. Over the last ten years, he had done a very good job of cleaning up Cedar Falls. It had the lowest crime rate than it had ever had in the last thirty years. The only thing Vargas did not do was clean up his own back yard.

Alec opened the door to the patio. "Hello, Sheriff Vargas. I am Alec Haskell with the FBI."

"I know who you are." Kelly said. "I have been expecting you. What can I help you with?"

GOVERNMENT

The two agents pulled up to the corners of the house and waited. Kelly saw them come up in his peripheral vision. "Sheriff, you have some evidence you gleaned from the backyard of the Methodist Church plus some personal effects of Pastor Goodman. I am here to obtain that evidence. I will need to prime your investigation."

"Please sit down, Agent Haskell. I still have all that evidence. At first, I thought I would destroy it, but I changed my mind. Then I thought I would just hide it, and I changed my mind again. I don't have it at my office, however. It is behind my seat in my truck under the carport. Here are my keys if you want to unlock it and get what you need."

Vargas had rolled over so easy that Alec could not believe it. He motioned to his agents to come get the keys and search the truck. As they were walking to the truck, he noticed some kind of remote on the patio table. "What is that....?" he started to ask. Suddenly, he hollered out to his agents to stop. Again he said to Vargas, "What is that on the table, Sheriff?" He reached out to get it and Kelly hit the button.

"B-O-O-O-M! As soon as the Sheriff had hit the activation button, the truck blew up into smitherens. Half of the house went with it. The agents were knocked twenty feet from the corner of the house, but they groggily got up. Blood was everywhere for they were cut with shrapnel from the truck and pieces of brick and mortar from the house. But, they were alive. Before they could regain their composure, Vargas took off running for the woods. Alec took off after him. He didn't get 50' before Vargas turned and began shooting at him with his 9 mm police issue Glock. All four shots missed Alec. Alec dropped down to his knees to make himself as small a target as he could. He drew his pearl handle colt .387 revolver, held it with both hands, shouted to Vargas to drop his weapon, and Vargas fired again knicking Alec in the arm. This time Alec fired with sureness as the pro he was. Vargas immediately fell to the ground. He was stone dead for the bullet pierced the center of his chest. Alec jumped up and ran to check on his agents. They seemed to be ok. "Let's go check on Mrs. Vargas inside," he said. They all three streamed through the back sliding glass doors. Mrs. Vargas was slumped over in her wheel chair. Brick and metal had pierced her head and chest. She was dead. "Ok, guys, how are y'all now that I've got a moment to ask."

"We are fine chief."

"Good, call the EMT's and get them over here to take these bodies in. It's been a long day."

As they walked back outside, Kelly had managed to get back on his knees. He was not dead as supposed. He raised his gun to fire, and one of the agents shoved Alec aside, drew his pistol and let go four fast rounds. Kelly slumped to the ground, this time for good.

"Well, I guess this all saved the taxpayers a lot of money not having a trial. And, what a waste. He did a lot of good for this community, but he couldn't keep his pants zipped up. Too bad about poor Mrs. Vargas. She probably didn't have a clue what was going on, and the pure innocent one out of the whole ordeal. You guys go inside and search his house anyway while we are waiting for the EMT's. We still have an active search warrant, and we might as well use it."

Both agents took off to the main bedroom. They opened the botton drawer of Kelly's chester drawers and let out a holler. "We found it chief. We found all the evidence we needed. We've got the knife, the totem with the gargoyle, four small human skulls, and an assortment of some mind altering drugs such as marijuana, hashish, cocaine, crack, heroin, some hallucinogens, inhalants and prescription-type psychiatric and opioid drugs used without a prescription. Man, this guy was into everything." They also found a letter from Pastor John Goodman dated a week ago. His return address was on the envelope. "We've hit the jackpot, Chief. This letter is instructing the Sheriff to dispose of all the evidence. I think we can safely extradite the good Pastor now....." And before he could finish his sentence, a noise sounding much like startled crows began to fill the air. Turning toward the woods where the sound was coming from, the three agents witnessed approximately 20 huge black ugly creatures lifting off into the horizon with a blood curdling SCREEE as they sailed out of sight. "What in God's name was that, Chief?'

Alec hesitated to answer. He had heard Buck and Jimmy talk about some creatures that looked like Gargoyles, but he thought they were having religious illusions. Well, if they were, then he was, too. "We will talk all about those creatures later when we have some experts tell us about them. But, know this, I think they are part of the problem around here."

Sheriff Vargas was dead, but it didn't matter to Alec. He had the evidence he was looking for and all he had to do now was get it to forensics, get some kind of idea what possible scenario went down, get extradition papers and haul Pastor John Goodman back to Cedar Falls. His ass is mine, he thought. And I don't care if he is a pastor, if he killed those kids, I'm going to see to it that he gets the death penalty.

5
ECONOMY

Farley Metzinger was the local stock broker. He had his Series 7 brokerage license and he could handle most any securities trade. His office consisted of three rooms, a waiting room, a secretary's office, and his office. It was located on the second floor of the bank building in downtown Cedar Falls. He had one secretary, Connie Blackstock who had been with him for 15 years. Connie was very reliable in her duties, and kept the office running efficiently and friendly. Farley's wife, Suzanne was a beautiful woman who had been a high school cheerleader, senior favorite, and had kept herself very well over the years. She could easily pass for 15 years younger than she was. When she had her hair up in a pony tail, she easily looked like a high school teenager.

Farley loved his wife and two kids, but he had one problem. He was over sexed. Often, during any given week, Connie would help him with his drive. Farley made plenty money. In fact, he was a millionaire. He had purchased Connie a condo and a new Mercedes. Suzanne was clueless to all these transactions, and considered Connie to be a friend and asset to Farley's business which she was, but she had no clue Farley and Connie had been having an affair for the majority of years Connie worked for Farley.

The day had been relatively slow. Farley didn't have any appointments, and Suzanne was off shopping. He got up out of his chair, went to the office door and locked it. Connie knew what was going to happen next. Farley walked behind her desk and began to rub her shoulders. Afterwards, he quickly got up, and went and unlocked the door. Suddenly, Suzanne appeared as if out of nowhere, walked in vibrant as usual, but stopped at mid room. Connie had been trying to put her panties on, but only got one foot in. All she could do was pull her dress down, and kick the panties to the side. The desk did not go all the way to the floor as most desks, but was a mod design that went half way down. Her panties were clearly evident, but she couldn't do anything about it. From Suzanne's viewpoint, though, she couldn't see at that moment. All she noticed was a flash of movement. She just assumed she must have startled them by the way she quickly entered the room. She said hi to Farley, greeted Connie, and said, "I was in town shopping, but thought I would drop by to say hello since my next stop is only a block away." Farley gave her a big hug, and she turned to leave. When she did, she noticed something wadded up at the corner of the desk. She kept walking thinking it may have been a rag, but after she got out the door, she realized it was a pair of nylon panties. How odd, she thought. Immediately, she turned and went back through the door she just came out of. Connie had just picked up the panties, and was standing there like a cow looking a new gate when Suzanne walked back in the door.

"What is that in your hand, Connie?" she asked.

Connie was totally flabbergasted and could not talk. She sputtered, "Uh, uh, uh. I was dusting off my desk."

"Baloney," Suzanne hollered. She reached out and grabbed the panties and yanked them out of Connie's hands. "Somebody please tell me what the devil is going on here, as if I don't already know."

"It's not what you think, Suzanne," Farley said. "She really was trying to dust off the desk. We just didn't have any rags to do it with, so Connie improvised."

"You can feed that king of crap to your clients, but you can't convince me. Looks like I interrupted you two because you might have your pants on, but your britches are still unzipped, and your underwear is slightly hanging out and wet besides. You want to try explaining it all again."

"Look, it got slow around here and we got carried away, but nothing happened, I promise."

"Bologna again. Connie, you have been here for 15 years. Exactly how long has all this been going on? The whole 15 years?"

"Well, not exactly."

"Ok, then y'all have been getting it on for 14 ½ years then. Farley, you sorry no count, you can book it, I am suing for divorce. And you are paying for it all. Y'all can go mess with each for the next 15 years if you want. I'm done."

With that, Suzanne stormed out the door. Farley and Connie just stood there with red faces and their mouths wide open. Farley knew Suzanne meant what she said. In fact, all the years they had been married, he never heard her use swear words, ever. Obviously, she was furious. In college, Suzanne studied law, and sat for the bar exam and passed. She just never practiced law because shortly after marriage, they had kids, and she wanted to be at home with them. Farley made good money and there was no need to have extra. Farley knew her knowledge of the law would ruin him financially. She would not need to seek out an attorney because she could well represent herself.

Within the week, Farley got his divorce papers delivered by courier. He knew it would be bad, but he didn't know it was going to be this bad. Somehow, Suzanne found out about the condo and the Mercedes he had purchased for Connie. It was still in his name, so Suzanne sued for that in the settlement. She also wanted the house, all its contents, their vacation home in Florida, her Jaguar, and ½ of his money and securities which amount to $2.4 million and sole custody of the kids with Farley getting no court ordered visitation rights. He was at the mercy of Suzanne if she wanted them to see him or not. In addition, she wanted $20,000 per month for child support and alimony. But, all that was not the killer for Farley. His brokerage firm was an LLC or partnership in which Suzanne was ½ owner. She was suing for his half of the ownership. Farley thought he would be ok, but found out Suzanne was studying for her brokerage license. She could fast track everything because she was so smart, and by the time the divorce was final in one year, she would have all the licenses she would need to run the business. Farley would have to start all over somewhere else, but it certainly wouldn't be Cedar Falls. He knew the judge in town, and that he was a righteous man, and would likely rule in favor of all Suzanne's requests, especially considering the circumstances and long term unfaithfulness of Farley. As far as he was concerned, his life was ruined. But, he still had $2.4 million and his car and clothes. He could start over.

Connie, on learning she was going to lose the condo and the Mercedes put the bite on Farley to get her another home and auto. He refused. She, too sued. When would this nightmare end, he thought?

Farley was renting space in the bank building. After the bank manager, Ben Biddle heard about everything that was going on, he approached Farley one day.
"Farley, I'm afraid you are going to have to leave your office here. It has come to my attention that you have been carrying on an elicit affair with your secretary for quite some time now, and that a lot of your sexual encounters have been here in the bank building. Such activities are totally impermissible and will not be tolerated here in this building according to our lease agreement. You have one week to relocate."

Ben left Farley in a huff, went to his office, said to his secretary Penny, "I need to give you some dictation. Bring your pen and pad, and close the door behind you."
Penny jumped up, got her pen and pad, headed straight to her bosses' office, and closed the door behind her. "Do you need some coffee or anything before we get started," she asked?
Ben's office was on the third floor of the bank building and was opulently decorated in the most modern décor. All the chairs and sofas were the finest leather, and he had mod art on the walls. His executive desk was clear except for his laptop set to one corner. He had a very nice credenza behind him with floor length windows on each side overlooking the main street of Cedar Falls. At one edge of the credenza was a small totem with a gargoyle on top.

Ben quickly jumped out of his chair when Penny entered. She was truly a "Deep Throat" kinda woman, he thought. After they finished, Ben said, "Now, let's take some dictation." Penny was an excellent secretary, and was exceedingly proficient in shorthand. Ben began to dictate the proceedings that had gone on between him and Farley that morning, and how Farley had broken the lease by his inappropriate actions. He would also report that he had a great tenant to take his place immediately. All of this was to be presented to the board that was going to meet Wednesday. They would want to know why one of their best paying and long term tenants was leaving. Ben had to be prepared for their questions.

What was not known is that Ben had a favorite cousin who had just gotten his securities' license, and he would be renting a prime space at a sweet heart deal. Ben already had it figured out that because Mason Franks had a different last name from his that none of the board members would be the wiser. It was bank policy that those next of kin to employees could not be employed at the bank because of possible conflict of interest.

Downstairs in the lobby, there was a lot of banking going on. Megan Pastorek, one of the tellers was busy fielding customers, cashing checks, making deposits, working the safe deposit boxes, answering the phone, and a host of other duties. Ben had hired Megan because she had a shady past, and he thought he could manipulate her to do some unseemly things. She was trying real hard to get her past behind her, but it seemed to follow her everywhere she went. It appears she had been working at a small hardware store at the cash register, and had stolen some money, sold some hardware at cost to certain customers, and even walked out the store on several occasions with some real nice equipment without paying for them. When she got caught, the store owners liked her so well that they wouldn't press charges, but wanted her to make restitution. Of course, after leaving the store, she never did. When Ben found out what she had done, and what she was capable of, he hired her especially since she had no criminal record on file anywhere.

Ben set up a dummy bank account with 30 social security numbers from deceased clients. They would have retirement and social security checks deposited electronically to this dummy account. It was easy to work out because the bank managed their estates and of course, Ben was the trustee. Nobody was the wiser. The only other person to know was Megan who had to make sure any inquiries got handled, funds were diverted properly and accounted for and pertinent letters from the bank as manager of the accounts was sent to the right places. All he had to do was cut Megan in for a fourth of the proceeds. And that was easy because Megan loved money among other things. Over the last 5 years, he had netted around $1 ½ million. It was a slick plan and nobody was the wiser.

Ben was passing by Megan's teller window on the bottom floor. She did not have a customer at the time. He went up to the window and said, "Come to my office around 5:30 this evening. We need to talk about a couple of things."

"Ok," she said.

Like clockwork, 5:30 rolled around and Megan entered Ben's office. Penny had already gone home around 5:15. "Yes sir, what do you need, Mr. Biddle." Ben grabbed her as she neared the desk.

"Oh, Mr. Biddle, what on earth do you want?"

It was that sense of power and wealth that makes people do things they would not ordinarily, but Megan accommodated him.

Penny walked in and saw them getting at it like a couple of rabbits. "What is going on here? She exclaimed. They both tried to stop, but they were in the middle of the act.

"You, SOB, I was just with you this morning and you just can't get enough, can you? I thought I was the only one. Don't bother getting your clothes on. I just came to pick up my glasses I left on your lamp table." She grabbed her glasses, and stormed out the door.

"Looks like we are done for," Ben said.

"Yep, it looks that way. There is no wrath like a woman's scorn."

The very next day, Ben got to the office a little late around 10:00 in the morning. He was the CEO, so he could come and go much as he pleased. As he walked up the stairs, he saw Penny coming out of the board room on the second floor. She whisked by him without saying a word. Ben walked into the board room where 4 of the 5 board members were sitting around the conference table. One of them had a light blue blouse and skirt in his hands looking at what appeared to be stains.

"Come in, Ben," they said. "We need to talk to you."

Buck Merriman had large security holdings at the brokerage firm and always kept $200,000 in his personal bank account plus CD's and IRA's. He visited the bank building a couple times a week to transact business. He walked into Farley's office only to find him putting papers and desk items in boxes.

"Where are you going, Farley?"

"Well, I am moving to another location. I think I have outgrown where I am now and need to expand."

For some reason, that statement didn't ring true to Buck. Farley had an unlimited clientele for he drew from cities and towns that were up to 100 miles away. He had a great reputation as a securities broker. "Farley, you seem cast down. Your bottom lip is lower than a snake's belly in a wagon rut. What else is wrong?"

Farley busted out crying. "Buck, I have sinned big time. I'm going to lose my business, my money and all my possessions, my wife and kids....why, why, I'm going to lose everything. I just don't know what to do."

"Hold on Farley, let's think about this. In the first place, the most important thing you think you might lose is your wife and kids. You named them last. They should have been first. You may need to get your priorities in order."

"Buck, I thought you might sympathize with me. Instead, you are berating me. We've been friends a long time."

"Farley, If what you can see is out of order, so is what you can't see. How do you stand with the Lord?"

"You know, Buck, I go to church every Sunday with my family. I tithe and give beyond 10%."

"Farley, you did not tell me how or what your relationship is with the Lord. Tell me plainly, are you saved or are you going to Hell?"

"Buck, I'm going straight to Hell for sure. I've been having an affair with my secretary for 15 years, and I have the most beautiful wife and children in Cedar Falls. In addition, I have put people in stocks and securities that they didn't need because I wanted the bigger commissions. I feel really bad."

"But do you feel bad enough to repent of your sins, Farley? Do you feel bad enough to repent and ask your wife for forgiveness? Do you feel bad enough to break it off with your secretary no matter what happens to you and your wife? Do you feel bad enough to repay those you have robbed? Tell me now, will you give your life to Christ and follow him?"

Sobbing and snotting, Farley cried out, "Yes, Yes, Yes, a thousand times yes to all of that. I want the Lord to help me. I repent of all my evil. Help me, Lord!"

"If you meant all that, enter into the joy of the Lord. The kingdom of God has now come to you. You are saved, you are changed, you are a new creature in Christ. You have been born again. Glory!"

"I feel it! I feel Him! I feel Christ in me that is! I have never felt so clean. Glory!"

"Farley, I am not going to tell you that you will get your wife, your kids or your business back, but I will tell you that you have just possessed your soul."

"What else do I have to do?"

"Absolutely nothing! You do not have any laws to obey. You have been saved by grace through faith. That is all that is required. Congratulations, my friend. And welcome to the Kingdom of God."

6
ARTS

Fred Stennet was the Manager of the local Cinema. It was the only movie theater in town. Early on Saturday morning, he was in his little 8'x8' office surrounded by pictures of scantily clad movie stars, porno, and billings with B rated movies hung around his walls. He is looking at some porno movies on his I-Phone, and begins to please himself. He sits there with the greatest sense of self release while at the same time wiping up the mess. Thoughts of bringing this type of joy to his customers fills his mind. Suddenly, out of nowhere an icy chill fills the room. He looks around to see if someone entered, a door opened, or if a window was ajar. Nothing. Again, the icy chill blew across his desk and rustled some papers. Startled that it happened a second time, he jerked to the side and knocked over some things onto the floor. As he reached down to pick up the scattered objects, he saw his favorite gargoyle totem laying there. A wing had been broken off. He picked up the rest of the papers and desk ornaments and began looking for some glue to fix the totem. He found some Gorilla Glue in his top drawer and immediately began to fix his prize display. It didn't take long, and it was all back in one piece. Proud of his work, he stroked the totem like someone would pat a Buddha's belly. It seemed to empower him to do more work. As he rubbed the totem, he felt a presence brush against his cheek as if whatever it was, was pleased with his repair job. He smiled! I have to get the movie schedule ready for the next month of days, he thought.

Looking over the list of new releases, he selected one PG13, five R rated movies, and one X rated movie. There were no restrictions in Cedar Falls for the first amendment was firmly in place. It was a patriotic town and folks didn't like to challenge their constitutional rights. It never occurred to him that a large percentage of folks might have community standards that would reject the X rated movie if it ever came to a vote. He also had an animated movie for the kids that had nudity, violence, and death. You can't start too young to indoctrinate these young minds, he mused. After all, nearly all had video games that were more evil than any of the movies he had available. Besides, the local coven would need some nubile girls ready to give away their virginity to the black arts. And, he really liked the young ones given for sacrifice.

About the time he started to look at the potential movie list, his door suddenly opened. It was Buck Merriman.

"Howdy, Fred. Hope I didn't interrupt anything important. One of your ushers told me you were here and that I probably could see you before you got started good. You got a minute?"

"Sure, come on in." Fred was glad he had cleaned up his mess, but his pants were still damp looking. Best not stand up, he thought. "What do you have on your mind, Buck?"

"Look, I know you are always looking for new movie debuts, and I have one that was just released that the whole town could see."

"And, what might that be?" Fred asked.

"It is a movie named "Klondike" and it is about a family of pioneers going west in the 1800's to look for, mine, and pan for gold in California. Greed has hit, and they with a multitude of others set out and will do nearly anything to find and stake their claim. Once they get out there, calamity hits and their daughter gets ill and almost dies. A preacher hears of their story and goes to pray for the daughter. Suddenly, she is healed after being near death. The family is so humbled, because the most precious thing, their daughter was almost taken from them, and she lives. After talking it over with his wife, and praying themselves, they decide that the most precious treasure they can mine is their children. Gold no longer held sway over them. He set up a general store in one of the boom towns, and made a fortune selling tools, equipment and supplies to the miners. Soon, they start up a home prayer meeting, and on telling their story over and over, a revival breaks out amongst the fortune seekers. Is that a tremendous story or what, Fred? And, it is available to bring here for at least two weeks. I believe it will be a box office hit, and it is ready to ship this day."

"Hold on, there, Buck. I already have a schedule of movies on order, and I don't have anymore available theatres to show it. Let's wait till later after it has been out for a while and see how it does nationally. We can always do it later."

"Ok," he said disappointingly.

Buck heard someone laugh. He snapped his head around to see what it was. Then, he saw it. The Gargoyle totem on Fred's desk. It was like it was glaring at him. A chill ran up his spine. Be not afraid of sudden fear, he thought. He got up to leave, grabbed the door knob and opened the door. Pffft, a rush of wind went through the door. And then he thought back of the Gargoyles he had seen, the totems people had owned, and most wicked and evil coven he had observed. Surely, Fred is not involved in any of this. He has always been so nice, he thought. But, so were the others who got involved. They, too, were upstanding citizens and leaders in their fields. He became wary of Fred, immediately.

In the meantime, Joe had a call from the museum. The director, Maxine Dalrymple. Maxine had a pretty good leak in her roof at the Museum, and it was damaging some of the artworks. He needed to get that roof fixed ASAP. As soon as Joe walked in the entrance of the Museum, there were moans and howls exiting the building. Maxine was walking across the floor to meet him, and collapsed right in the middle of the building.

Joe went over to pick her up. "Ms Dalrymple," he said, "everything is going to be alright."

She looked up, reached out her hand to catch his, and said, "What happened?"

"You fell. That's all."

"But, I feel like all my strength is gone. Did I faint?"

"No, Ma'am, your power left your body."

"I don't understand. My power left my body? How can that be? Did I deplete my electrolytes? Have I had a heart attack or a stroke?

"None of things, Ms. Dalrymple. The darkness within you has left. The spirits that empowered you are gone."

"Are you talking like spirits, do you mean demons? Before you were born, your mother dabbled in the dark arts. You were possessed from your mother's womb."

"How do you know all these things? Are you a prophet or something?"

"I tell you that when light is come, it will dispel all the darkness. I am the light of the world. You will never again be oppressed by darkness."

"All my depression is gone. It was so bad, I was near suicide on several occasions. I feel alive again, and I mean right now. I haven't been this free feeling in years. In fact, I have never felt like this. I always wanted to, but I never knew how to get there. Look, I don't know who you really are, but I am glad you came by. I read a lot, and I try to read the Bible, but it was always so difficult. I do know Christ in the Bible cast out devils. And, as I appreciate what I read, there were those that said only God could do that. Are you God or the Messiah?"

"I will tell you that you are not far from the Kingdom. Only the spirit of God could reveal these things to you. Be blessed. Now, where is that leak?"

Maxine went dancing and skipping to the location of the leak. She always wanted to do this as a kid, but she was afraid others would laugh. She knew this was the beginning of a whole new way of living. Oh, and this carpenter made her come alive. He doesn't look like God, in fact, he looks a little like a college dropout, OH WELL, she thought. And, she did another little jig.

Rene' Cologne was a director in another local coven and he was a movie film maker. It was his dream to film one of the Satanic rituals, get all the blood and sacrifices, and sexual orgies on tape. The only problem was nobody in the coven wanted to be filmed. It could be very incriminating and maybe lead to jail and prison terms. Rene' was also bisexual. He really loved women, but he had no problems getting it on with men.

The thought occurred to Rene' that if he could get Curtis Rinauld, the head of the Dance Team at the University and who was a known to be an out of the closet homo, and Liz Chamberlain who was the head of the College Beauty Pageant to lend him some of their students, both male and female that he could re-enact a coven meeting. Then it would all be play acting and no one would be the wiser. He knew plenty women himself who went to the casting couch in the movie business, Liz would know the beauties who slept with the judges, and Curtis would know every homo and lesbian on the dance team. He was going to need some very perverse subjects to do this movie. Besides, he thought, they might make some good black magic for real later once they got a taste of the dark side.

Rene' walked into his opulent office, passed his desk to this credenza, rubbed his totem Gargoyle, and reached for the phone. "Curtis, this is Rene' Cologne with Cedar Falls Movie Studios."

"Sure, Rene', what's up?
"Look, I'm planning on making a horror movie about Satanism, and I need some of your students who might be interested. Some of the scenes will be full nudity, sexual orgies, and blood rituals. I will need kids who can go both ways if you know what I mean."
"I think I can arrange that. How many do you need? Actually, let me re-phrase that. I think I can get around 20 or so that might do something like that."
"Great! I'm having an audition Saturday morning at 9:00 AM at my studio. Have them there then. You come, too if you like."
"See you then."

Rene' then called Liz Chamberlain. "Liz, this is Rene' Cologne."
"Hey, Rene'! I haven't heard from you in a month or so. How are you doing?"
"I'm all good. Look, I'm going to make a movie about Satanism, with rituals containing full nudity, sexual orgies, and blood sacrifices. Do you have any girls that is in or have been in the beauty pageants that might be interested in having a part?"
"Hey, yeah, I have a few. In fact, I might be interested as well. I have never been in a movie. Sounds like fun. When are you going to start?"

"Saturday morning at 9:00 AM at my studio. We will do auditions then. Do you know where I am located?"

"I sure do. And, I will have as many gathered up as might want to. See you then."

Rene' could not believe his instant success in getting a cast for his movie. The coven members can go screw themselves. These kids will all be better looking, have great bodies, and project better on screen. He already had a script ready made for such a movie, and he was thinking this was going to be a great success.

Buck Merriman and Jimmy Hawkins were having an early breakfast together Saturday morning. Chuck Driscoll and Anita Beckstrom walked in about that same time and they greeted one another.

Anita said, "Mr Merriman, did you know Rene' Cologne was holding auditions this morning at his studio to interview a scad of people for his next movie. It is one on Satanism. The reason I know is that he called me and asked me to be a part. I am pretty sure he knew I was in a coven and had participated in activities in it. In fact, he is in another coven on the other side of town. No one is supposed to know about it."

"What?" Exclaimed Buck. What is the nature of the auditions, Anita, if you don't mind me asking?"

"Well, I think they are going to do some nude scenes and practice some orgies to see who they can keep and who they have to cut."

"Are there any minors in it as far as you know?"

"He asked me. I'm still 17. I think he is getting the majority from the beauty pageant contestants and the dance team troupe at the University. They should all be over 18. I know he made some other phone calls. Some of the girls that were in the coven with me were as young as 15. I'm not sure if he called them or not. I know the ones going are excited about being in a movie. They don't care about what it is or what they have to do."

"Jimmy, we have to go do something about this, especially if there are minors involved."

"Hey, I want to go," chimed in Chuck.

"Ok, come on, but it might get a little hairy."

Chuck was big and tough, worked out on weights all the time, and was an on fire for the Lord at all times.

"I can cast out devils if need be," Chuck piped up.
"Yeah, and you might make a pretty good body guard as well."

Off they went to Cedar Falls Studios. They were parked outside the building about a quarter till nine when people started arriving. We will wait until a little after nine before we start in. Get that camera ready on your Iphone, Jimmy. We may need some evidence. About ten minutes after nine, they started to the front door. You would know it, it was locked.
"Let's go to the back door."

They started to wind there way down a narrow alley full of dilapidated movie sets, old equipment, and just plain junk. When they got to the back door, it was locked, but the door had a lot of crack between it and the jam. Jimmy said he thought he could get his knife in there and unlock it. It was a snap. The door came open. It entered into a storage room with another door to the main studio. It had a small dirty window on it. Buck looked through the window and saw about 30 kids all nude milling around, while some were engaged in some kind of sexual activities. He tried the handle. It was not locked.

"Get up here with your phone and take some videos first, Jimmy. We might not be able to get these shots inside. I think I see three or four minors. Make sure you get them in the video. And, I will step back outside and see if I can get Stephen's buddy, Alec Haskell from the FBI to come over if he is still in town. We might need some type of police intervention."

Buck stepped out to make the call, but never got it dialed. He heard a ruckus inside. Someone obviously had seen Jimmy videoing at the window and had opened the door to see who it was. A scuffle ensued. The phone was knocked out of his hand, and the kids scattered. Not even one was left inside. Buck opened the door and saw the phone on the floor. The window was cracked. Jimmy was on the ground with a big gash on his head. Chuck was standing over him trying to pick him up.

"Thanks for that big right hand, Chuck," he said. He could have hurt me worse if you had not been here. Buck looked at the phone. It didn't look good. It was pretty badly damaged and it was not on. Not a good sign.

"Here, Jimmy, see if it still works."

Jimmy hit the on button. It powered up. He immediately went to the video app and hit play. "Yeah," he said, "it still works. The only problem is the screen is so cracked you can't see anything with clarity."

"Let's get it over to Alec. We may need some professional help. Hopefully this is going to be Rene's first and last Satanic video.

Alec was able to take the phone apart, get the chip, and put it in some sophisticated equipment and view everything on a wide screen.

"Wow," Buck exclaimed. "I had no idea you could do that."

"Do you recognize anyone in the video, Buck or you Chuck or you Jimmy?" Alec asked.

They all answered at once. "We sure do."

"Ok, then, give me all their names that you know, and we will look their addresses up. I will need Rene's address as well as those aiding and abetting including Maxine Dalrymple and Curtis Rinauld. Sex with a minor itself is rape and is a felony offense. They can all get long terms in prison. In addition, we can get them for sexual exploitation of a minor, child sexual abuse, and child pornography. They won't see light for a long time. Way to go guys! Y'all hit a home run with this one. And, for the most part, we stopped it before it got started."

7
MEDIA

Paul Decelle was the newspaper manager and chief editor of Cedar Falls Daily News. He had one fault. He would write anything for a headline that would sell papers. And he always had. As soon as he heard Buck had stirred things up at the movie studio, he was at his door looking for a first hand interview. Knock Knock!

Buck came to the door. "Hey, Paul. What brings you to my home?"

"Buck, I got it straight from a college kid that you got some news for me. Like catching some of our leading citizens with their clothes off with some minors. Mind if I get a story?"

"Paul, there were minors involved and for that reason I can't talk to you about it. It might jeopardize the case. Alec told me to keep everything under my hat till we get definite depositions, inform the juvenile authorities, and parents of all the minor kids."

"How many were there? Minors I mean?"

"There were several. But, that is really all I can tell you. Look, I know you really want to get a story, but it is just too early to report it. We need to wait." Buck, slowly closed his door. "See you later, Paul. Bye!"

Paul was not about to be denied. He knew a couple of the college kids at the scene. Now if only he could find them. He went out to the student center called the "Totem Pole" at the University and started asking around. The kids were more than glad to tell him what they knew and where and who the kids were in the audition. They would tell him anything if only they could get their names and picture in the paper.

One of the college students named Susan came to him, and said, "Mr. Decelle, my name is Susan. I heard you were looking for information about the movie Mr. Cologne was making. It was about Satanism. But, I have the real thing if you are interested."

Paul paused a minute. "What do you mean the real thing?"

"I know about a real coven on the East side of town that no one knows about. It has been kept secret for 50 years. It has some of the more prominent citizens of the community involved such as judges, attorneys, business men and women, chamber of commerce directors, investors, and you name it. They are in it. If you are interested?"

"I sure am! Give me some details."

"Well, as I said it is on the East side of town located in the middle of 100 acres. It has a fence all around it and is heavily guarded. They do Satanic rituals there and a high amount of drugs."

"How do you know about it?"

"When I was 15, I thought I wanted to be a Satanist. I was talked into going to one of the rituals. Next thing I know I'm strapped down to a table and I'm raped by 20 different men. I lost my virginity that day. And, I have never been the same since. I got pregnant and had to go back regularly until my baby was born. On the 8th day after birth, they sacrificed my baby girl to the God of Darkness. They slit her throat, caught her blood in a silver chalice, and all drank so they could be empowered to do black magic. I threw up all over the place, and have never been back. They threatened me with death if I ever told about any of this. Now, 4 years later am I only able to talk about it. I have been so depressed ever since. I have wanted to commit suicide from that date. Help me!"

"I will, Susan. First, tell me where this place is. I have never heard of it and I have lived here for 20 years."

"I can tell you exactly where it is if you can help me. I don't want to die. And they said they would kill me if I ever told. You have got to protect me somehow."

"Ok, I know I need to get you some asylum first. Let's go see Buck Merriman. He knows an FBI man here who can provide that. Then we will talk about where this place is. But, I want first rights to the story. Deal?"

"Deal!"

Buck saw Paul coming a 100' away. He was prepared for him, but not prepared for what he just heard and what Susan told him. "Paul, we can do this, of that, I am confident. Let's get Alec Halsell on the case. He is the pro. And, he has the power to put those suckers in jail."

After calling for over an hour, Buck finally got Alec on the phone. "Alec, we may have the 'motherload' here. I have Paul Decelle of the Cedar Falls Daily Newspaper and a college student named Susan who says she knows of another coven on the East side of town in the middle of 100 acres with wire fencing and armed guards. I think we may need a lot of agents on this one."

"I will be there in 30 minutes. Hold tight."

In about 30 minutes, Alec drove up in his big black Chevy SUV. He screeched to a stop, hopped out, and said, "Give me the whole scoop. I have a stenographer here to record everything."

"Susan began to rehearse her story to Alec that she told to Paul. Paul said, "Tell me where this place is located."

Susan told him the same thing. "First, I have to be protected and get some kind of asylum. Those people intend to kill me. And, if they ever find out I told, they will certainly kill me."

"Ok," said Alec. He motioned to one of his deputies. "I want a 24 hour armed guard for this young woman from this day forward till we get all these clowns behind bars. She is very valuable to us, and we can't afford to lose her. Got it?"

"Yes, sir! I got it."

"Ok, are you ready to tell us what you know, little lady?"

"Yes, sir. The compound is located 20 miles out of town on Highway 70. You take a left on a narrow asphalt road called Styx Street. Go about

5 miles and take a right on the only dirt road to the right. In about 1 more mile, you will come to a 20' gate, a guard house with 3 guards with military style AK 47's, and a perimeter fence around the 100 acres with a half dozen Doberman's inside. Inside, the gate about 100 yards away is a Mexican styled mansion. It is surrounded by guards front and back. It is a 2-story building with a big meeting area. Guards are on the stairs, the balconies, and nearly all the rooms. It would seem impenetrable to me. In front of the mansion or compound is a huge 50' totem with a giant Gargoyle on top."

"Are you serious? It's got a Gargoyle on top?"

"Yes, sir!"

"Buck," Alec chimed, this may be the biggie. It could be the bust of the century. If this place has Satanism and drugs, it's got prostitution, money laundering, illegal contraband, and maybe a whole lot more. I'm going to get 50 deputies out here ASAP. It may take them a day, but I can fly them in with this one. In the meantime, we can plan a strategy. I think I can get some GPS and video satellite imaging of the compound with the description Susan gave us. Maybe, we can get some names discreetly, of course. Susan, you have been in the compound. Do you remember or know of any of the people in it."

"I know quite a few."

"Ok, somebody bring me some paper and a pen. We need to make a list."

The next day, Alec's men arrived around 11:00 AM. He had some of the best agents and SWAT team on the planet as far as he was concerned. They came with full battle gear, weapons, and armor. The unit commander approached Alec. "We are ready, Chief. What is the plan?"

Alec had gotten the best surveillance maps and pictures available. He laid out the plan how they would surround the compound, make sure there was plenty of meat for the dogs so they would not bark, cut holes in the wire fence at strategic places around for entry, then just before dawn, swoop down with an intense raid before everyone got up. He knew after being with the force for over 20 years, even the best laid plans could go wrong. Everyone was on high alert to activate the plan and prepare for contingences if necessary. They had the element of surprise on their side.

Alec had an Apache chopper fully loaded with 50 caliber guns and missiles if necessary. The plan was to take everyone alive if possible. That night, they began to drive out to the compound in unmarked cars spread out so as not to draw attention to the raid. They were careful to drive by the turn off if any other vehicles happened to be behind them or approach. There was a section of woods on the dirt road. They would pull off in these woods, hide their vehicles, and walk the mile up to the compound. There was no moon out, so they were practically invisible with their dark SWAT suits on. They could hear the dogs in the distance, so there should not be any disturbances that was not already seen to. Four men went to the sides of the fence, threw the meat over, and the dogs were totally satisified. They had plenty more besides in air tight bags if necessary.

The team moved up surrounding the compound. They shot the two guards at the gate from 50' away in the woods line with tranquillizers. They were down instantly without a sound. Two of the agents put on the guards coats and stood sentry so if any one was looking, everything would appear normal. Fifteen agents went in the front gate. Holes were cut on every side of the fence for the rest of the agents. Guards on the perimeter fence were also brought down with tranquillizers. Easing up to the sides of the compound, they were able to take guards out at the door just as easily. So far so good. With grappling hooks, eight agents scaled the sides of the compound and got on top. They found a scuttle beside the heliport for air passengers. The surveillance photos were perfect. It was still dark and entry had been made to the house. Everyone was still asleep. At a preplanned signal, Agents rushed through every room, yelling FBI. You are under arrest.

All the guards were handcuffed, and some of the fine upstanding citizens of Cedar Falls who spent the night for the Satanic services the next day were all subdued and put under arrest.

After everything was secured, Alec walked through the building getting evidence. There was a huge basement room where they were making crack cocaine by the tons. On one end was tables piled up with money. In the millions, Alec could only guess. A double door led into another room which had a huge arms storage. Every kind of weapon imaginable was in that room. After taking pictures, Alec went upstairs. In the main meeting room, it was set up for a coven meeting much like the barn on the west side of town. There was a totem with a Gargoyle, a stainless steel sacrificial table, pentagrams, candles, mattresses, and every kind of satanic tool and symbol imaginable. Again, he took pictures.

He went upstairs and found several bedrooms with huge round beds in them all highly decorated. On the walls were photos of nude girls of various ages, some in single shots and some in sexual positions with different men. Alec called Buck upstairs to see if he recognized any of the people in the pictures. He did. A lot of them. Many leading citizens of the town. On the walls were stacks and stacks of videos. Cameras and TV's were everywhere. Popping in a few tapes revealed they were all porno films. One entitled "Nubile" had several underage girls, some with hardly any breasts at all, meaning they were very young, maybe 12 or so. Buck knew a couple of them.

It looked like the raid was very successful. Alec had his men confiscate everything in the house. They had to get big U-Hauls it was so much.

Buck said, "I have one more job to do. You know that big ole' totem outside with that giant Gargoyle on it?"
"Yep!"
"I'm pulling my truck up to it, hook it to my electric winch, and I am pulling that sucker to the ground. Then, I am cutting it up and burning it like firewood."

By this time, the townsfolk had heard about the raid. A lot of prominent citizens had been arrested. Chuck pulled up to Jimmy Hawkins' home, told him about what was going on, and asked if he wanted a ride to the compound. Of course, he did, so they hopped in the truck and took off. They could be there in about 25 or 30 minutes if there was no traffic. On the way, they saw Joe, the carpenter walking down the road, stopped and told him about the goings on, and asked if he wanted to go. He was glad to ride.

Buck called Paul Decelle. "Paul, you were the one to break this story and you need to have the exclusive. Get in your car, come out to the compound, and watch me pull the totem down."
Paul exclaimed, "I'll be right there."

They all met at about the same time. Buck told them to gather around the totem. "We are going to pull this monstrosity down to the ground, then we are going to burn it. Chuck scaled the totem, and tied the winch cable up close to the top. He went about half way down and tied a trailing cable hooked to the winch. Buck had a 100' cable so he had plenty room to bring a 50' totem down. Chuck shinned down, and stood around with the rest of the witnesses. This was going to be a momentous moment.

Buck began to engage the winch. He pulled it up tight, then put it in low gear. The totem looked like it might break, but the cable about half way up held. Over, over, over. Bammmm! It hit the ground with a thud.
Suddenly, as if out of nowhere, the sky filled with Gargoyles. They were screaming and making sounds like crows in torment. The screeching was a horrendous sound. Thousands lifted up and began to fly away. Buck broke out his chain saw and began to cut the totem to pieces. The guys piled up the wood. As soon as it was cut up, Buck threw diesel on the wood and set it on fire. Gargolyles swooped at the little group of heros trying to claw and bite whoever they could. But, out of the sky, Gargoyles began to fall to the ground. Chuck hopped on a 4-wheeler and went and picked one up. He was huge. He had at least an 8' wing span. But, he was dead. Something about the fire burning the totem destroyed their power and life.
Then, Buck grabbed the Gargoyle which topped the totem. I have been saving the best for last he said. He broke off it's wings and head, and put the body and wings and head in the fire which was by now burning with great intensity. Gargoyles started to fly back at our heroes.

Joe held up his hands, and yelled, "I bind you Satan!" Again, Gargoyles all fell to the ground dead.

Alec just stood there in unbelief. In all his life, he had never witnessed anything like this. Paul was busy taking notes, dictating, and videoing the greatest event he had ever seen.

Buck opined to Paul, "Paul, you get the greatest scoop of your lifetime. I wouldn't be surprised if you didn't get the Putlizer Prize for Journalism. You really broke this ring right up. It just goes to prove that the pen is mightier than the sword. Kinda' like the Bible, isn't it?"

After the tumult was over, the ashes had died down and the last Gargoyle breathed its last breath, they all started back to their trucks to head back to town to see who all was in jail. Alec's deputies had hauled all the evidence back with them, had some upstanding citizens in cuffs, rounded up the guards of the compound, and went to town with a list of people to arrest.

Amazingly, as they all drove back in their trucks, they sensed the greatest peace as they entered town. The usual chaotic atmosphere was gone. It was a month till Christmas, and the streets were filled with happy shoppers. Four groups of carolers were on street corners and in front of churches. The town had a gala mood.

Joe got out of the truck, walked around and shook everyone's hand, and said, "Welp, I have to be on the road. I have things to do in other places."

As he walked out of sight, Buck was the first to speak. "He certainly was not your typical Charismatic. Everytime I got around that guy, my heart would burn inside." To this everyone immediately agreed.

IT WAS GOING TO BE A VERY MERRY CHRISTMAS

Printed in the USA
CPSIA information can be obtained
at www.ICGtesting.com
CBHW051930221024
16238CB00015B/879